D1264017

The Music of the French Psalter of 1562

———

NUMBER THREE OF THE
COLUMBIA UNIVERSITY STUDIES
IN MUSICOLOGY

PSEAVME XXIII CL. MA.

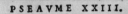

Il chante les biens & la felicité qu'il a : & d'une merueilleuse fiance se promet que Dieu, duquel ce bien luy vient, le traitera tousiours de mesme.

A PAGE FROM THE PSALTER

The Music of the French Psalter of 1562 · A HISTORICAL SURVEY AND ANALYSIS · WITH THE MUSIC IN MODERN NOTATION

By Waldo Selden Pratt

Published on Morningside Heights in the City of New York · · *1939* · *by* COLUMBIA UNIVERSITY PRESS

THE AMERICAN COUNCIL OF LEARNED SOCIETIES HAS
GENEROUSLY CONTRIBUTED FUNDS TO ASSIST IN THE
PUBLICATION OF THIS BOOK

COLUMBIA UNIVERSITY STUDIES
IN MUSICOLOGY

BOARD OF EDITORS

Foreword

"THOU SHALT compass me about with songs of deliverance." "I will sing praises unto my God while I have any being." That unparalleled treasury of religious lyrics known as The Book of Psalms contains many such expressions as these. It is hardly likely that we shall ever know surely the music which was sung to such words in the days of the royal singer, David, and of the other poets who contributed to this marvellous anthology. But the poems have never ceased to exercise their magic on the spirits of men since they were first sung.

When Christian musicians raised their timid voices in the early centuries of the Church, they drew largely from this well of inspired song. The beginning of the development of the liturgical books of the Christian Church rested upon an arrangement of the Psalter for regular use in worship. When the restless spirit of reform troubled Europe in the 16th century, the Book of Psalms was again pressed into service, in the languages of various peoples and in a metrical form fairly close to the folk spirit, to be the vehicle of the musical expression of religious fervor.

Professor Pratt's scholarly exposition and minute analysis of the musical aspect and quality of this form of religious expression in the church of Calvin makes it clear that the wealth and variety of rhythm, of meter and of melody displayed in the music of the French Psalter does not fall short of the rich and varied beauty of the poetry of the original. The wide-spread influence of the collection, greater even in other countries than in France, and the lasting qualities of some of the tunes, used even in the present day, may be explained in part by the fact that a gifted poet, Clement Marot, and a wise and skilful musical editor, Louis Bourgeois, watched over its

Foreword

early beginnings and established a model for its later development.

Professor Pratt's illuminating commentary, supported by a meticulous, systematic tabulation of the results of formal studies, offers to English readers the possibility of a closer acquaintance with a phenomenon highly significant not merely in the field of psalmody and hymnody, but in a much wider range of general musical interest.

OTTO KINKELDEY

Cornell University
December, 1938

Preface

THE STUDY here presented was at first not a definite project, but an unplanned sequel to other lines of inquiry. It grew out of efforts through many years to gain basis and background for practical teaching, without thought of publication. Only as results accumulated and were commended as important by sundry scholars was an exposition of them in print undertaken. It was felt that the methods used and the conclusions reached should be made available in definite form for consultation by other students.

The music in the French or Huguenot Psalter is by no means unknown. Yet its intrinsic interest and its historic significance are not commonly well understood except in a limited circle of European experts. Much has been written about it in various ways. But little of this is in English. Even the full musical contents of this Psalter are not readily accessible. Hence many references to it are clearly inadequate and some seem incorrect. Such defects of knowledge or judgment are most unfortunate in view of this Psalter's obvious historical importance and its close connection with the spread of the Reformed or Calvinistic branch of Protestantism as distinct from the other branch known as the Lutheran.

The central feature of the present study is a complete rescript in modern notation of the one hundred and twenty-five melodies in this famous Psalter. To throw these melodies into proper focus there must be added a considerable amount of historical or technical annotation. Up to a point the superb work of Douen on *Clément Marot et le psautier huguenot* (Paris, 1878–79, 2 vols.) furnishes a wealth of documented material, most of which is here freely utilized. But even his treatment fails fully to deal with all the significant details.

[ix]

Preface

The text of the tunes as here given is primarily taken from a beautiful copy of the Paris edition of 1562, but has been checked by comparison with a variety of later editions in French and with several versions in other languages, especially Dutch, German, and English. The substantially exact preservation of the French melodic tradition for fully three centuries is remarkably impressive, as is also that of the Dutch tradition (identical with the French) for a like period. No thorough effort is here made to indicate the minute variations from these standard traditions that may be found in such adaptations as have been made for German or English use, though some comparative remarks are made at various points.

The series of melodies is reproduced in full musical notation. But in the technical discussions—both to save space and to facilitate rapid reference—considerable use is made of other symbols that are less common. These latter, it is hoped, will be sufficiently clear for scholarly use. They are carefully explained in Chapters VI and VII.

Though this study is historical in aim, its artistic implications cannot be missed. The 16th-century tunes sprang out of the musical life of their time and attained place and influence for artistic reasons. Among them the French collection had a remarkably wide acceptance and has shown an exceptional persistence as a whole. In it are many melodies that in figure, movement, and harmonic fitness are not far from modern feeling. That but a scant two or three of them have commonly been preserved in English and American usage seems to be due not to any lack of artistic quality, but to the curious working of literary and other prejudices.

Without attempting to enumerate all the persons and institutions whose interest has made the completion of this study possible, the writer owes a peculiar debt of gratitude to Dr. Otto Kinkeldey, Dr. Percy Goetschius, and the late Dr. Charles N. Boyd, together with the Case Memorial Library in Hartford, Connecticut, for constant and invaluable assistance.

Hartford, Conn.   WALDO S. PRATT
November, 1938

Contents

PART I

The Psalter as a Whole

I

Early Protestantism and Its Use of Popular Song

AMONG the salient events that made the 16th century famous
was the beginning of the complex movement usually known
as the Reformation. We need not here take space for any discussion
of the main reasons or causes of this movement—some of them
reaching far back in the centuries—or for any summary of its large
consequences or results as they confront us even today. Macaulay
was doubtless right in saying that "if Luther had never been born
at all, the 16th century could not have elapsed without a great
schism in the Church." [1] Yet the movement would not have attained magnitude and importance without able leadership. All those
most active in its inception were ecclesiastics in the Roman Church,
and their initial purpose was reform within the policy and practice
of that Church rather than separation from it. But their protests
were not welcomed by those then in control of the Papacy, so that
the situation promptly developed into hostility on both sides. Hence
came not only a demand for a general purification of morals among
both clergy and laity, but the planning of new systems embodying
restatements of doctrine, readjustments of ecclesiastical polity, and
fresh types of liturgical practice. Our present inquiry lies in this
last field for the most part, though it has connections with the
others as well.

It was inevitable that the new movement should pursue differing
paths, dependent on the personal and racial elements involved and
on the political and social conditions within which these elements
found themselves. Thus Protestantism in leading countries like
Germany, France, and England, even though moved by more or less
related purposes, tended early to adopt notably independent and

---

[1] *Essay on John Dryden*, 1828.

[3]

even divergent forms. We need not here dwell upon the contrasts between these national forms or their partial interblendings. Yet we cannot avoid marking the separation between the German and the French evolutions, despite their contiguity and some likeness in their political surroundings. It is usual to ascribe the separation to a disagreement in doctrine. Yet account must be taken of essential diversities between racial temperaments and between racial ways of thinking and habits of social action. Due weight to these latter is especially called for in such a topic as here lies before us.

For our present purpose, certain facts in the complicated story need be recalled. In 1517 two distinct reactions against the existing ecclesiastical system occurred almost simultaneously. One of these was in Saxony under Martin Luther. The other was in Switzerland under Ulrich Zwingli. The occasions in the two cases were not quite the same nor were the two proponents acting in concert. Both aimed at the reform of certain abuses and both remained at first in the historic Church; but both were driven by resistance into active independency. Luther's influence quickly enlisted the aid of several powerful German princes to such a degree that the supremacy of the Pope and the Emperor was threatened. Zwingli's fiery zeal, however, effected little at first except to divide the Swiss cantons into opposing groups, which remained at war for more than ten years. While acting as chaplain in these conflicts, Zwingli himself was killed in 1531. His views had meanwhile spread somewhat into France. And thus Geneva, being on neutral ground and readily accessible to French refugees, soon became the headquarters of "The Reform," as the movement began to be known. Though other leaders—such as Farel and Bucer—were not lacking, decided progress awaited the accession of John Calvin about 1535 and his recognition as leader at Geneva in 1542. The two types of Protestantism, therefore, though beginning almost together, came to maturity in succession, the Lutheran some twenty years before the Calvinistic. As time went on, Lutheranism spread widely in Germany and into Scandinavia, while Calvinism ranged rather in Switzerland, France, the Low Countries, and Great Britain, besides penetrating into Germany at many points. Both types have remained vigorous in one or another form, not only in their original habitats, but in distant quarters of the globe.[2]

In the present study we are mainly concerned with a single usage that was characteristic of all the Protestant bodies, though in detail more or less peculiar to each of them. This usage was the congregational singing of versified texts to appropriate melodies. Such singing had at times been a feature of Roman practice, but had become extremely rare, though decidedly common in secular life. All the reformers sought to link it afresh with religion, their object being to afford an outlet for the expression of personal experience and to promote a solidarity of sentiment among all who made up an assembly. The habit of such song became at once a badge of adherence to the new faith, and it also proved a powerful implement in spreading that faith and in binding together all classes, high and low, into a sense of fellowship.[3]

To meet this need, manuals of song early began to be prepared and before long attained extensive circulation. The first book in German came out at Wittenberg in 1524, the first in French at Strassburg in 1539, and the first in English (derived from German sources) about 1539. In all of these the basis of the poetical text was prevailingly Biblical.[4] But from the first a difference of method appeared between the German and the French developments. The German instinct chose to give voice rather to personal experience, while the French confined itself to reproducing the Psalms and

[2] The literature about the Reformation is too vast to be noted here. See brief summaries in various encyclopaedias, or such a general survey as that in Williston Walker, *The Reformation*, New York, 1900.

[3] Much valuable information as to the genesis of popular sacred song in Germany is given in Edward Dickinson, *Music in the History of the Western Church*, New York, 1902.

[4] The German book was *Geystliche Gesangk Buchlein*, Wittenberg, 1524, by Luther and Walther (though preceded by Bohemian books from 1501). The French book was *Aulcunes pseaulmes et cantiques mys en chant*, Strassburg, 1539 (no editor or printer named), to which reference is made in Chap. II. The English book was *Goostly Psalmes and Spiritualle Songes*, about 1539, by Coverdale. This last, known only in a unique copy at Oxford, was based wholly on German sources and had no wide influence. See article in John Julian, *Dictionary of Hymnology*, 2d ed. 1907.

other poetic passages in the Bible. Thus the growth of German church song led more toward what we now call "hymnody," that of the French rather toward "psalmody," the latter tendency remaining emphatic until after 1700. Ultimately, the distinction became unimportant, since the poetic impulse was basically the same and the musical treatments adopted were analogous. At first there was difficulty in securing competent poets to supply suitable texts. It was not long, however, before the literary material became abundant. It has gone on increasing, so that now the register of Protestant hymns in all languages is of enormous extent.[5]

The plan of structure of both verse and music was largely derived from that found in the popular songs of the period. The verbal texts, that is, were cast in metrical feet and corresponding lines, so that, by means of accent and length, of pattern and rhyme, a certain number of lines should make up a stanza more or less complete in itself. Successive stanzas were alike in structure, so that a single melody could serve for the whole of any one poem. This type of metrical and stanzaic verse had long been known among ecclesiastical poets who wrote in Latin and had been instinctively chosen for secular songs in the vernacular of various countries. But its structure had not much influenced the practice of professional musicians, whose interest centered more upon the traditional plain-song and its contrapuntal elaboration. During the 16th century, however, the ecclesiastical and popular lines of musical method began to interweave and combine, bringing to pass a gradual, but significant, transformation in musical style. By 1600 something like the plasticity and emotional expressiveness of modern music was plainly visible. The solo melody had gained full recognition, along with the chord-relations that distinguish modern harmony (including the rudiments of modulation), and important progress had been made in rhythmic and metric formulation. Thus by that time the way

---

[5] See especially Julian, *op. cit.*, which ranges widely over many languages, and L. F. Benson, *The English Hymn*, New York, 1915. In the German field, reference should be had to the notable works of Wackernagel, Winterfeld, Koch, Tucher, Zahn, Kümmerle, Wolfrum, etc.

was opened not only for large vocal forms like the opera and the oratorio, but for a variety of purely instrumental forms as well.

Early in this process of transformation came the striking vogue of Protestant church song, sweeping through more than one of the leading European countries. This had no conscious motive of artistic reconstruction; it simply reflected the spirit of the age. But the ardor that went into it and the immense range of circulation that it attained doubtless made it more of a positive and determinative factor than is usually conceded for it by historians.

We are not called upon here to discuss the many topics in debate at the outset of the Protestant movement or to trace out its evident interconnections with sundry intellectual and social agitations of its day. But some rapid remarks may well be made about the environment in which the movement advanced and about the two conspicuous leaders who gave it its character.

Though the 16th century opened in the midst of the signal awakening known as the Renaissance, the main traditions and institutions in force everywhere were those of mediæval feudalism.[6] What we now call Germany was then a tangled maze of states, large and small, each under a ruler who held proprietary power over all his subjects. France had been likewise somewhat divided, but was emerging into at least a nominal unity. The latter's political status was made difficult, however, not only by its long-standing competition with England, but especially by the extension of Spanish dominion into Flanders on the north, into Italy on the south, and into Austria on the east. The incessant struggles for control of the so-called Holy Roman Empire and even of the Papacy itself accentuated the general condition of instability. Hence Protestantism, though in essence not at all a political enterprise, was beset on every hand by a complex of intrigue and conflict. In northern Germany the situation was on the whole favorable to the new faith, while that in France was mostly adverse. A critical factor in its early

---

[6] The word "Renaissance" has been given more than one meaning. It is here used as a convenient term for the period of perhaps a century from about the middle of the 15th century. See article by J. A. Symonds in the *Encyclopaedia Britannica*.

progress was the quality of its chief directors, each in relation to the innate racial character of the peoples involved.

The two great leaders seem in many ways to stand in decided contrast. Luther, sturdy in body, ardent and aggressive in temperament, was mentally versatile and alert, shrewd and magnetic in dealing with men of every station, capable of warm sympathies and also of strong antipathies, not unready to yield minor points to win success with essentials. His whole life, whether as monk, as theological professor and author, or as diplomat and controversialist, was marked by devout and heroic earnestness. He had the skill and good fortune to draw to his side many helpers and supporters of great worth and influence. Thus he made an appeal of permanent intensity to the Teutonic readiness for united action under bold and energetic leadership. Calvin, on the other hand, never robust and often disabled by ill-health, was apt to seem austere and aloof, though he was by no means wanting in sensibility. His strength lay in his disciplined and solid scholarship, his keenly logical and critical faculty, his fixity of conviction and unswerving determination, his far-sighted genius for organization. During his most active years he seems to have had few real assistants—perhaps because of his liking to act alone. His primary field of influence was upon the acute and individual mentality of the Gallic spirit—characterized by an instinct for precision and order, for discrimination and system, and combined with a capacity, when fully roused, for passionate devotion.[7]

In the French field the Roman Church was firmly entrenched. It is remarkable that in it Calvinism spread as fast and far as it did, since, unlike Lutheranism, it was mostly unsupported by large political units, but was disseminated chiefly through individuals and by means of correspondence and publication. From its base in a corner of Switzerland Calvinism moved at first westward into southern France and northward into the upper Rhineland. It leaped over into Holland, where presently it was adopted as the religion

---

[7] The above brief reference to the contrast between the two great Reformers is, of course, far from adequate. It simply emphasizes certain points that occur in subsequent pages. For further remarks about Calvin see Chap. VIII.

of the state. It also gained the confidence of small groups of sympathetic adherents in many other Continental countries, such as Italy and Spain and the more distant Bohemia, Hungary, and Poland, while making a more definite and progressive penetration into parts of Germany. During the bloody reaction in England that culminated in Mary's reign (1553–58) many British Protestants took refuge at Frankfort and Geneva. There they acquired ideas and impulses that bore fruit in the Calvinistic elements in the doctrine and liturgy of the incipient Anglican Church, besides becoming regnant in the Kirk of Scotland and thence in the strong Puritan party in England. It was from these British sources that most of the early settlements in America derived their persistently Calvinistic character.

In France, meanwhile, the new faith, though often punishable by death, gained such headway, both among the nobility and in the artisan and peasant classes, that before Calvin died in 1564 its adherents constituted a formidable party in the state. Hence came astonishing vacillations of royal policy at Paris. At times the Huguenots—as they now began to be called—enjoyed governmental concessions and even periods of control. At other times they encountered such violence as to be forced into civil war, including in 1572 the savagery of St. Bartholomew's night. Under Henry IV the Edict of Nantes (1598) ushered in a period of partial and nominal toleration, during which the Huguenots prospered and multiplied. But in 1685 Louis XIV revoked this Edict, offering the entire Huguenot population the grim choice between recantation, flight, or death. The most of them, probably several hundred thousands, emigrated, largely to Holland, England, and America, and Huguenotism as an organized force came to an end on French soil. The expulsion of the Huguenots was a greater loss to France than to Calvinism. Long before that event Calvin's influence had stretched far beyond France. So it comes about that the churches that are Calvinistic in some sense now many times exceed those to which Calvin himself originally ministered.

Much of the momentum of early Calvinism was due to the

patience with which Calvin gathered his convictions into scholarly order. Even before avowing himself a Protestant he had framed the outline of his monumental *Institutes* (first issued in Latin in 1536 and completed in French in 1559). This summary of doctrine rested upon acute and original Biblical studies, such as later he demanded of his pastors and teachers, for whom he wrought out commentaries on the whole New Testament and on Genesis and the Psalms. Involved with this system of thought was a scheme for church organization and government, which became typical of the polity known as Presbyterian. Calvin also gave careful attention to the details of public worship, including some things that his followers have forgotten. It is in this last field that we find his determined interest in psalmody. The cultivation of verse and song, he felt, was essential for congregational worship and also for private and domestic devotion. Doubtless his mind dwelt first upon the Scriptural words, but he also recognized the power of poetry and melody to make words vital and memorable. Zwingli, who was expert in music, had hesitated to use it in worship, while Calvin, who was not musical, aimed to magnify it.[8]

To many minds much in Calvin's doctrinal thought—especially as this is often interpreted—is not now satisfactory. His plan of polity, also, is not the only one that has proved effective. But his emphasis upon congregational prayer and praise has validity even now, though not always remembered in churches of his order. Even those who do not accept all he taught on these various subjects must acknowledge the vigor and sweep of his reasoning, the pertinacity of his zeal for truth, and his masterly skill in building up a great system of thought and action.

[8] In addition to Calvin's collected *Works* and *Correspondence,* see a notable summary of his liturgical projects in C. W. Baird, *Eutaxia, or the Presbyterian Liturgies,* New York, 1855 (enlarged as *A Book of Public Prayer,* 1857). The first edition was revised and reprinted in London by Thomas Binney in 1856. These books are valuable because they include much about other Reformed leaders besides Calvin. See article about Baird in Schaff-Herzog, *Encyclopaedia of Religious Knowledge,* New York, rev. ed., 1891, Vol. IV.

II

The Rise of French Psalmody

THE EARLIEST declaration of Calvin's purpose to nourish church piety and worship by means of the singing of Psalms seems to have been made during his first sojourn at Geneva. In January, 1537, he and Farel submitted a memorandum to the City Council in which was a definite proposal upon this subject.[1] This led to nothing at the time, since Calvin's leadership was not yet established and a year later he was forced to betake himself to Strassburg. There for four years he served as pastor for a small French congregation that found itself surrounded by strong Lutheran churches where song had been in use for at least ten years. Hence it came about that the first songbook in French was drafted in Strassburg in 1539, certainly with Calvin's knowledge and approval, whether or not under his direct editorship. To this pioneer book we shall return in a moment.

Mention of this book brings up a point that needs to be constantly remembered in our discussion: namely, that the completed French Psalter of 1562 was the culmination of a process of develop-

[1] Here and in later pages constant reference is made to the great monograph of O. Douen, *Clément Marot et la psautier huguenot*, Paris, 1877–78, 2 vols. The text of Calvin's memorandum is there given in I, 278–89. Douen had the advantage of freely using the researches of Félix Bovet, *Histoire du psautier des églises réformées*, 1872. Thus his work supersedes various German works of earlier date, such as Winterfeld, *Der evangelische Kirchengesang*, Leipzig, 1843–47, 3 vols.

All later discussions are necessarily dependent on Douen. Aside from sundry pamphlets and books in French, to which reference is made elsewhere, certain summaries may well be mentioned here, such as six articles in *The Musical Times*, London, 1881, by Major G. A. Crawford; a paper in the *Proceedings of the Musical Association*, London, 1907–8, by Rev. G. R. Woodward; three lectures at Princeton Theological Seminary in 1917 by Rev. Dr. L. F. Benson (the leading American hymnologist), later printed in the *Journal of the Presbyterian Historical Society*, Philadelphia, 1919; and various articles in *Grove's Dictionary of Music and Musicians*, latest ed., London, 1927–28. The present writer has published two brief articles on the importance of the French Psalter as a historical monument, one among the pamphlets of the Hymn Society, New York, 1932, the other in *The Musical Quarterly*, New York, 1935.

ment that had been going on for almost thirty years, passing at first through a stage of experiment, and subject to the influence of more than one personality. It is also to be remembered that this development had two aspects, distinct, though intertwined. One was essentially literary—the provision of versified verbal texts. The other was musical—the provision of melodies or tunes suited to make these texts singable. Our present concern is with the music. But proper attention is also required for the poetry, since this dictated the form of the tunes to a considerable extent.

The completed Psalter is often called that of Marot and Beza, since the text was wrought out wholly by two poets—in this respect being unique among the early books of its class. The two authors were Clément Marot (c. 1497–1544) and Théodore de Besze or de Bèze or, as Latinized, Beza (1519–1605). These two men were separated in age, in social rank, and in intellectual interests. Apparently they never met. They stand linked together in history solely by the fact that in succession they served Calvin's determination to furnish a manual of congregational song for his widening circle of followers. Marot had the more evident poetic genius and much greater experience and renown. But Beza, who also had for a time some poetic aspiration, was a trained scholar and endowed with greater concentration and capacity for sustained effort. Both men commanded the confidence and support of Calvin, though Marot was directly associated with him for but about a single year, while Beza became his trusted assistant in many undertakings and was ultimately his successor in the leadership of the Reformed movement.[2]

The beginning of Marot's translation of Psalms seems to have had no conscious relation to the use to which they were finally put. In 1532–33, having been for at least fifteen years a favorite and pro-

[2] Douen devotes 14 chapters to Marot and 2 to Beza. Marot's biography is usually treated in leading works upon French literature. Many collections of his poems have been published from 1544 to 1884. Beza's life has also been often described and his theological works collected. A good short account of Marot is found in the *Encyclopaedia Britannica* (by Saintsbury), and one of Beza, in Schaff-Herzog, *op. cit.* For further notes on both men, see Chap. VIII.

tégé of Francis I at Paris and of his sister, Marguerite d'Alençon (later Queen of Navarre), Marot conceived the idea of turning some of the Psalms into French verse—somewhat as he already had done with many poems in Latin and Greek—even seeking some knowledge of Hebrew to aid him in the task. As the number of his paraphrases grew and became known in the court circle they aroused a singular furore of interest, largely because so few knew the contents of the Bible. Though not at first published, they gained informal circulation outside the court, among all sorts of people and even in places far away from Paris. Inasmuch, however, as they were renderings of Scripture into the vernacular, they brought the poet under increasing suspicion and constraint. Finally, when at length they were published in 1542, though bearing the royal *privilège* and having been commended by the Emperor Charles V, they led the authorities to indict the poet for heresy, so that then he had to flee for his life to Geneva. His first collection included versions of thirty selected Psalms. At Geneva, under Calvin's urgency, he completed nineteen more, besides renderings of the Nunc dimittis and the Decalogue.[3] After about a year, however, he left Geneva for Savoy, where at Turin in August, 1544, he suddenly died—possibly, as some have thought, a victim of poison.

For five years after Marot left Geneva Calvin was baffled in finding any poet fitted to carry Marot's work to completion. But in October, 1548, Beza arrived at Geneva as an unexpected accession to the ranks of the Reform. Within a year his sincerity and ability were so evident that Calvin laid upon him the remaining task of versified translation. By 1551 Beza had thirty-four Psalms ready and by 1554 apparently seven more. All these were immediately published (though the editions varied somewhat in completeness), being regularly combined with the whole series by Marot, so that the total

[3] Marot's first collection included Pss. 1, 2, 3, 4, 5, 6, 7, 8, 9, 10, 11, 12, 13, 14, 15, 19, 22, 24, 32, 37, 38, 51, 103, 104, 112, 114, 115, 130, 137, 143. The order of composition is not known, except that Ps. 6 was the earliest, apparently because it is the first of the 7 "Penitentials" (all but one of which occur in the above list). His remaining versions (1542–44) are Pss. 18, 23, 25, 33, 36, 43, 45, 46, 50, 72, 79, 86, 91, 101, 107, 110, 118, 128, 133, with the Nunc dimittis and the Decalogue. See table in Douen, I, 305–6.

number varied between eighty-three and ninety. During the next few years Beza filled in the sixty versions required to cover the whole one hundred and fifty poems in the Psalter, so that in 1562 the entire collection was ready for issue. In this about one-third is by Marot and two-thirds by Beza.[4]

Whatever may have been the reactions between two such dissimilar personalities as those of Marot and Calvin, it is notable how promptly the latter adopted Marot's earlier versions and how urgently he sought for more. In the case of Beza the same relation was repeated and rapidly intensified. For Beza had legal, linguistic and logical training that fitted him to be a lieutenant and colleague in a much more extensive degree.

It is usual to rank Beza's share in the text of the Psalter as inferior to that of Marot. Yet tribute is due him for the steady fidelity and zeal with which he labored to maintain and expand the standard which Marot had set up.

At this point we may well add a reference to the singular bibliographical problem as to the first stage of Marot's work, as well as to the music that was linked with it. So far as we know, he did not publish his first thirty Psalms until early in 1542 (at Paris). Later in that year Calvin also published them (at Geneva). But prior to these are three other extant books that are plainly related to them. These were as follows:

1. *Aulcunes pseaulmes et cantiques mys en chant,* Strassburg, 1539. No author, editor, or publisher named. Contains 13 Psalms of Marot, though much altered (1, 2, 3, 15, 19, 32, 51, 103, 114, 115, 130, 137, 143), and 6 others (25, 36, 46, 91, 138, 113—the last unrhymed), besides the Nunc dimittis and Decalogue in verse and the Creed in prose. A strange feature is that 5 psalms are numbered as in the Latin version (or Vulgate), while all the rest are numbered as in the original Hebrew. All the 22 pieces have melodies; but Pss. 114 and 115 are set to the same one. Of these 21 melodies, 16 at first were adopted into the French Psalter, 11 of

---

[4] Beza's first versions were of Pss. 16, 17, 20, 21, 26–31, 34, 35, 39–42, 44, 47, 52, 57, 62–65, 67, 73, 90, 111, 119–127, 129, 131–134. His later additions covered all not previously translated.

them permanently so. This book is known only through a unique copy at Munich.[5]

2. *Psalmes de David, translatez de plusieurs autheurs et principalle-ment de Cle. Marot,* Anvers, 1541, with double indication of Pierre Alexandre as editor and sponsor, he being a Carmelite in service to the Queen of Hungary (sister of Charles V and sister-in-law of Francis I), then governante of the Low Countries. Contains 30 Psalms by Marot, much altered (as in the Strassburg book), with 15 others (including some duplicate renderings) by writers indicated only by initials or abbreviations. The numbering of the Psalms is that of the original Hebrew throughout. No melodies are given, but 10 versions are referred to popular songs. This book seems unconnected with the Protestant movement, but, being a translation of the Bible into the vernacular, was technically illegal. Yet it was not at once named as such in the list of proscribed books. Hence the conjecture that its material from Marot was derived from some copy given by Charles to his sister. The changes in Marot's text were later repudiated by him. Some four or five years later Alexandre became a Protestant and his writings were publicly burnt at Brussels. From 1555, after a sojourn in England, he was pastor at Strassburg, from 1558 at Metz, and from 1561 again in London.

3. *La Manyere de faire prières aux églises francoyses . . . ensemble pseaulmes et cantiques . . .* 1542. Contains an Order of Service for Sundays (with prayers), 38 Psalms (2 in double translation) and 4 canticles, a Catechism, directions for Baptism, Communion, and Marriage. The texts of the Psalms and canticles correspond with those in the 1539 Strassburg book and the 1541 Antwerp book, those by Marot in altered form. The melodies given include all those of 1539, with 7 new ones, leaving 12 without music. Only one (Ps. 104) became permanent in the French Psalter.

At the end appears an extraordinary note—*"Imprimé à Rome par la*

[5] Two facsimile reprints of this rare book are available, one edited by Delétra at Geneva in 1919 and the other by Sir R. R. Terry at London in 1932. The latter transcribes both words and music in modern form and adds harmonized versions, set to English verses by Mrs. K. W. Simpson. Many of the annotations supplied are useful, though a few seem not fully considered. The main points of question are these: (a) The reference on p. i to the allegedly meagre treatment of the 1539 book by Douen hardly does justice to the latter's Chap. XII and to his giving in full 19 of its melodies in Chap. XXI; (b) The account on p. vi of the familiar confusion in the numeration of Psalms fails to note its origin in the Septuagint (copied in the Vulgate); (c) The many references to Goudimel's harmonies fail to date them from 1565 (Goudimel was killed in 1572) and to say that they were based on the final edition of the French Psalter in 1562; (d) The footnote to p. 81 overlooks the likelihood that Pss. 114 and 115 were meant to be sung to the same tune; (e) On p. 101 what is properly Ps. 91 is provided with an English rendering of Ps. 90!

Commandement du Pape," with a printer's name. This addition is doubt-less wholly false, as the book was probably edited by Brully, who followed Calvin as pastor at Strassburg, and published there. The note seems to have been devised by the printer to promote circulation among Catholics and was later repudiated. Hence the edition is commonly called "the Pseudo-Roman."

To complete the curious story, we add a note about the nexus between these three books and what may be called the "official" editions at Geneva.

Calvin returned there from Strassburg in September, 1541, and two months later was authorized by the Council to introduce the early Strass-burg Psalms into regular use. His purpose was aided in February, 1542, by securing the fuller Pseudo-Roman edition. Shortly after appeared a new Prayer Book with contents similar to this latter, though much re-modeled. The Psalms include 30 by Marot (still in altered form) and 5 possibly by Calvin. The latter was as yet unaware of Marot's authentic text, which he seems not to have known until Marot's arrival at Geneva in November, 1542, when, of course, he adopted it, thereby displacing the versions often associated with his own name.

The problem thus outlined seems insoluble unless new evidence can be produced.

Whence came the altered texts of Marot used in 1539 at Strass-burg, in 1541 at Antwerp, and again in 1542 at Strassburg? Whether there was a link through Charles V and his sister is purely hypothet-ical. Even if some transmission occurred, was the text then authentic or already altered? In short, was the corrupted text made in Ant-werp or in Paris? In any case, how did a set of versions made under Catholic auspices pass to Strassburg and become accepted for Protes-tant use?

Who really edited the 1539 Strassburg book and who prepared the versions there added? The versions may have been by Calvin, but the confusion in numeration—and also some printing errors in the tunes—seem unworthy of so precise a scholar as he.

The tunes in 1539 and 1542 all came from Strassburg and seem to have been inspired by Lutheran usages there. Yet few, if any, of them have been identified with Lutheran tunes then existing. It is likely, however, that Matthias Greiter, an able musician in Strass-burg and a Protestant since 1524, may have been concerned with them, as his name later is given in print with some of them.[6]

[6] Most of the points here given are from Douen, though not all of his conclusions are adopted. See also Théodore Gérold, *Clément Marot*, Strasbourg, 1912; and his valuable *Les plus anciennes mélodies de l'église protestante de Strasbourg et leurs auteurs*, 1928, in the latter of which is a notable biography of Greiter.

III

The Significance of the Completed French Psalter

THE BOOK of Psalms has always occupied a place of peculiar reverence. In the Hebrew Scriptures it usually stands first in the Hagiographa or Holy Writings that rank next to the Law and the Prophets. Its varied contents, often cast in beautiful poetic form and imagery, have appealed to Jew and Christian alike, to Catholic and Protestant, to the learned and the untaught, to those deeply devout and to those with mere literary interest or those groping after spiritual light. With the rest of the Old Testament, the Psalms were translated into Greek before the Christian Era in what is known as the Septuagint version.[1] Thence, much later, they passed into Latin in the so-called Vulgate translation. Still later they were rendered gradually into a multitude of modern languages, and have given rise to commentaries by the score or even hundred. In both the historic Eastern and Western Churches the daily use of the Psalms has been ordered in the Horologion of the one and the Breviary of the other. At the Reformation this mighty tradition was duly preserved to a large extent, especially in the churches of the Calvinistic group. Both Lutherans and Calvinists chose to magnify the method of translation into metrical and stanzaic verse, so as to adapt all the Psalms, when combined with fitting melodies, for general participation through congregational singing.[2]

Under the conditions of its origin, it was inevitable that this early Reformation song should unfold along three more or less distinct

[1] The Hebrew Psalter is undoubtedly a compilation (like a modern hymn-book). The problems of authorship and dating seem largely insoluble, in spite of the portentous efforts of scholars from ancient times to the present. See, for example, the summaries and bibliography in C. A. Briggs, *Commentary on the Psalms,* New York, 1906–7, and four articles by the present writer in the *Journal of Biblical Literature,* New York, 1913–14. In the Reformation time the Psalter was usually ascribed to David.

[2] See masterly summaries in Julian, *op. cit.,* under various headings, covering the pioneer work in both psalmody and hymnody in Bohemia, Germany, France, Holland, and England.

lines, in Germany, in France, and in Great Britain. These usages differed in language and somewhat in musical tradition, besides being representative of different types of ecclesiastical organization. Thus were laid three cornerstones for the later Protestant developments in hymnody and psalmody. These three were the series of German *Gesangbücher* from 1524 to Luther's death in 1546 and several years following; the French Psalter in its evolution from 1539 to 1562; and the two pioneer British Psalters as built up between 1547 and 1562 or 1564. Regarding the poetic texts of all these a large amount of information is accessible. But as to the exact number of the tunes brought into common use we are not so sure. Prior to 1565 we may assume that German melodies numbered perhaps 250,[3] the French total about 150, and the British rather less. The courses of the German and British streams have, until comparatively recently, been better explored and mapped than the French. Yet it is clear that the primary significance of the French Psalter is as a historic monument alongside of the others of its time.

A second significance of the French Psalter lies in the exceptional character of its poetic framework and of the music added to it. Here it stands in some contrast with its German and British relatives, since its texts were made by but two poets and its tunes mostly compiled or composed by but one musician—all these being experts. The result was a remarkable unity and intensity, so great that much of it persists unchanged to the present day. This significance, then, is that of intrinsic quality.[4]

To these must be added a third point. In breadth of circulation and in persistence of use in full, the French version may be called a literary phenomenon. Even its range of influence among the Huguenots was notable, in spite of the tempests through which they went for more than a century until their final disorganization in 1685.

[3] See Johannes Zahn, *Die Melodien des deutschen evangelischen Kirchenlieder,* Gütersloh, 1888–93, 6 vols., especially VI, 1–42.

[4] Douen has dealt elaborately with the poetic aspect of the French Psalter—far more than is necessary here. He has also gone into much detail about the tunes, especially on the side of bibliography. The aim of the present study is to carry his discussion further and to relate the French style of music to that of other countries.

Long before that event the impress of the French Psalter had far overleaped the boundaries of France and taken its place as characteristic of the Reformed faith in general. The respect paid to it was not merely temporary, but has proved singularly enduring, so that it belongs not only to old France, but in some sense to the wide Christian world. Upon this point we may well dwell here, at least enough to indicate its force.

While the French Psalter was still in the formative stage (before 1562) over 30 publications of portions of it were made, either with words alone or words with music. In 1562, when it became complete, there were at least 25 editions published, probably more. Between 1562 and 1599, when the Edict of Toleration came into effect, some 80 others were added. From 1600 to 1685, when this Edict was revoked, at least 90 more appeared. This makes about 225 separate publications during the formal existence of Huguenotism in France, not to speak of the many since 1685. There is no means of estimating how many copies in circulation these printings represent, but the total must have been several hundred thousands. And there may have been other publications of which we have no trace.[5] Huguenotism in France held its place for about one hundred and fifty years—five or six generations. The total number of its adherents during this time can hardly have been less than two million persons. Among all these the Psalter, accepted and conscientiously revered as second in value only to the Bible, was a precious possession, not only read, but memorized.

The above statement relates only to books in French. But the relations of Huguenotism to similar movements outside of France were remarkably many and close, not only while it was in formal existence, but in later times. Accordingly, the use and influence of the French Psalter were prodigiously extended through translations into languages other than French. Douen cites such translations into over twenty languages and dialects—Dutch, Flemish, German,

---

[5] Here and throughout Part I, the main source is the great bibliography in Douen, II, 503–621, slightly supplemented from published catalogues of the Bibliothèque National at Paris and the British Museum at London, etc.

English, Danish, Italian, Spanish, Portuguese, Swiss, Gascon, two forms of Old French, Polish, Bohemian, Hungarian, Slavic, Bantu, Malay, Tamil, Persian—besides Latin and Hebrew. In each case the Marot-Beza text serves as the basis, necessarily accompanied by the tunes. The Dutch version passed through some thirty editions and the German at least twice as many. All this points to an immense range of influence for the Psalter outside the land of its birth.[6]

The earliest of these translations was that into Dutch by Datheen in 1566, only four years after the French original was completed. This soon became the official manual of song for the Reformed Church in the Netherlands and so continues, though much revised and extended. This accounts for the translations made for Dutch colonies in the Far East and also for the initial usages in the Dutch settlements in America.[7]

The next translation of importance was that into German by Lobwasser in 1573. In spite of the opposition existing between Lutheranism and Calvinism from the outset, the latter penetrated widely into Germany and has remained active. Lobwasser's book continued in large circulation for at least two centuries. It had many interlacings with Lutheran books, receiving from them and giving in return.

[6] Means are not at hand for verifying this list in full or arranging it in chronological order. Some of these translations were evidently rather early, made to supply the needs of groups of churches outside of France or Switzerland which adopted the Reformed usages almost at once (several of these passing through perhaps several revisions later). Others belong as late as the 19th century, being due to the extension of missionary undertakings from France, Holland, or Switzerland. The latest that I have actually collated are the Dutch version of 1858 and the Malay version of 1855.

As an example of missionary expansion of tune-books, note that in South Africa, before the extension of British dominion, there were no less than eight editions of the standard Dutch version in as many dialects of the great Bantu language. See article in Julian, *op. cit.* (under "Dutch Hymnody"), by Dr. J. A. Hewitt.

[7] In 1773 an extensive revision of the original Dutch version was adopted by the Reformed Church of the Netherlands. This revision is said to be still in use in a few churches in the state of Michigan. Its tunes are almost exactly those of the complete French Psalter of 1562, except for a variant reading of one line.

The earliest use of the French tunes in America was by Huguenot expeditions to Florida and South Carolina in 1564–65 (preceding the founding of St. Augustine), where friendly Indians are said to have caught up the French melodies and continued to sing them long after the small settlements were wiped out by the incoming Spaniards (see C. W. Baird, *Huguenot Emigration to America,* New York, 1885, 2 vols., I, 65–77). The pioneer church in New York was organized jointly by Dutch and French settlers in 1628, the two parties having identical tunes for the Psalms, but with the words in their respective languages.

This explains the use by German musicians of some tunes of French origin.[8]

In England a complete translation from the French, with the music, was made in 1592.[9] This, however, had small influence. The main impact of the French usage upon the British came much earlier. During the Marian persecution, as already noted, from about 1550 a throng of British refugees fled to Frankfort and Geneva. There they became familiar with the ways of Calvinistic churches. Some of them had in hand the English metrical renderings of about 40 Psalms made by Thomas Sternhold (from about 1547), with a few others added by John Hopkins after Sternhold died in 1549, and were interested in building up a complete English Psalter parallel to that being formed in French. Details are lacking, but three partial Psalters in English were printed in Geneva in 1556, 1560 and 1561, ranging in contents from 51 Psalms to 87. These editions are collectively known as the "Anglo-Genevan Psalter." Several poets were at work. Some sought to follow the style set by Sternhold and Hopkins. Others chose to translate or imitate the French book of 1551. Through these latter, among whom were Kethe and Whittingham, and also through whomever acted as musical editor, a considerable and important direct nexus was set up between the French and the British Psalters.

After Elizabeth's accesssion in 1558 the exiles drifted homeward. There the process of forming a complete Psalter proceeded under two committees working independently, one in England, the other in Scotland, and led to the first English book in 1562 and the first Scottish in 1564. These two Psalters were largely alike in preserving the early Sternhold-Hopkins nucleus and in tending to other similarities, but the English adopted little from the Anglo-Genevan, while the Scottish took practically all in that version.[10] Hence the direct

---

[8] Lobwasser's edition (variously revised) remained standard for German Reformed churches till the middle of the 18th century. See Schaff-Herzog, *op. cit.*, under "Lobwasser."

[9] Douen had a copy of this practically unknown book.

[10] Regarding the Anglo-Genevan books, see Julian, *op. cit.*, under "Old Version," and the dissertations prefixed to Neil Livingston, *The Scottish Metrical Psalter of 1635*, Glasgow, 1864 (recently reprinted by Sir R. R. Terry in London).

impress of the French prototype was small in England, but large in Scotland. This impress was soon made indistinct in both countries by the debilitating tendencies in the form of both verse and music that came in with the 17th century. Indeed, the first Scottish Psalter was definitely displaced by a second in 1650, which acquired much greater popularity.

Much more will be said later as to the musical details of this whole process (see Chap. X).

While the above three points of significance of the French Psalter on its literary side are abundantly sufficient, it is not to be forgotten that the fact that both Marot and Beza were so much concerned in it has further significances. We will mention but two of these, confining ourselves mainly to Marot, since Beza belongs in a later time —not closely connected with that now in view.

The Psalter of these two authors played a part in the large awakening of French popular thought to the nature and richness of the Bible. Ecclesiastics, of course, had long known much of it from the Latin translation. But the popular mind could not be reached until translations into French were attempted. The pioneer versions of this latter sort were those of d'Étaples (1530) and Olivetan (1535), furnishing a basis for still better versions later. It was between the above dates that Marot was seeking some knowledge of Hebrew under Vatable, one of the progressive scholars at the Collège de France through whom Francis I was aiming to introduce a new life into French education. During the same years the boy Beza was living in the family of Wolmar in Orléans and from him gaining his first knowledge of Greek. In both cases we see at work a literary curiosity that was novel in France and which pointed toward a further inquiry as to what was in both the Old and the New Testaments—an inquiry which ecclesiastical authority was sedulously trying to prevent or stifle.[11]

We might linger, also, over the share which Marot had in the for-

[11] Regarding the rise of Biblical scholarship in France during Marot's life, see the many works on versions of the Bible, including Samuel Berger, *La Bible française au moyen âge,* Paris, 1884.

mation of French diction and style, though his work falls between the influence of the eccentric Villon earlier and that of the famous Pléiade a little later, as well as between that of Rabelais and Montaigne. Marot's influence came from his works as a whole, most of them having small relation to his Psalms. These latter constitute but an insignificant fraction of his poems. Yet they were among his last productions and represent his ripened skill as a word-painter and verse-maker, and their sincerity and warmth shed light upon that serious and noble side of his versatile mind that had not earlier always expressed itself so clearly and sustainedly. Being what they are and remembering their extensive circulation among all classes, from king, princes, and nobles down to the burghers and the peasants, these Psalms possess no small significance in the course of French literary history.[12]

[12] Francis I was but slightly older than Marot. His interest in the latter was nearly coincident with his project of founding the liberal Collège de France in opposition to the conservative Sorbonne. At his court, as later at that of Ferrara, Marot doubtless met most of those that were eminent in the progress of letters and the elevation of social life. Among these was surely Rabelais, who, beneath his rough and reckless satire, was a fertilizing literary force and probably a somewhat earnest critic of manners.

IV

The Versification and Meters

THE POINT of direct contact between the text and the music is in the exact form given by the poems. To this poetic form the tunes must be fitted with scrupulous exactitude. It is here that the French Psalter presents much that is remarkable, if not difficult to understand. Its extreme variety has always stood against its ready adoption or even appreciation by certain classes of students. Yet this variety was evidently chosen deliberately and has commanded acceptance in many other languages than French.

When Marot began his work he may have been somewhat influenced by poems or songs of his own time. But he was also familiar with all the manifold types of verse that had been cultivated in France since the long-past time of the Troubadours and the Trouvères.[1] In his early Psalm-translation he did not foresee the application to stated congregational use that finally was to be the outcome. Whether, if he had known, he would have wrought differently, we do not know. He was moved by a poet's impulse to wrap his thought in varied encasements, shifting with the emotional content of the Psalms themselves. This variety was emulated and even extended by Beza in his studious completion of what Marot had begun. All this multiplicity of form must have met with the approval of Calvin, who himself was not inexpert in verse-making.[2] And the event proved that it was also accepted by a vast public of

[1] Modern poetry owes much to the development of Romance versification, in which the Troubadours of Provence were pioneers. For summaries and biographies, see the article on "Versification" in *The New International Encyclopaedia,* New York, 1908.

[2] Calvin is known to have made versified Psalms in 1539, when he was 30 years old. In the Strassburg book of 1539 there are 8 poems not by Marot, but with no author given. Hence Douen and others suppose these to be by Calvin. But Bovet hesitates because of their heavy versification. This latter view is strengthened if one compares Calvin's beautiful "Je te salue, mon certain Redempteur," of which an English translation, in the fine original meter, is in Philip Schaff, *Christ in Song,* New York, 1868, pp. 678–80.

singers, not only in France, but in countries where these verse-forms were not germane.

To every metrical feature of the words the tunes were necessarily fitted—one tone, and usually but one, for each syllable.[3] Hence the musical editing was much more than a choice from existing melodies, but involved a studied invention as well. The prevailing aim seems to have been to make each Psalm individual in text and tune, something to be treasured in the memory and consciousness by itself. This aim at individuality is certainly achieved in both words and music. But the process is usually dictated by the verse.

The rhythm is mostly iambic, but with about a dozen deviations, usually into trochaic—the reverse of iambic. In both, two syllables make a "foot," but with accents differently placed.

But it is in the formation of stanzas that the French style is most exuberant. Stanza-form depends on the number of lines, their lengths and endings, and their grouping by means of rhymes. Every variation in any of these elements produces what is commonly called a "meter," whether applied to the verse or the music. In the 125 tunes of the French Psalter there are 110 different "meters," each of which demands a particular form of tune. Two-thirds of the stanza-forms have either six or eight lines, while one-third vary between four lines and twelve. The shortest line consists of four syllables, the longest of twelve or even thirteen, and every number between is represented (except eleven). The proportion of feminine endings (with the accent on the next to the last syllable, instead of on the last) is notably high—about three-eighths of all the lines. Masculine and feminine endings are usually mingled together in the same stanza, often with fine effect. The groupings by rhyme are varied, forming couplets, triolets, quatrains, and even longer metrical units.[4] In all these regards French usage seems to have outrun even the German. It stands in impressive contrast with the monotony long persistent in England.

[3] The only slurs in the music are in 2*d*, 6*a*, 10*g*, 13*d*, 91*bd*, 138*i*.

[4] A study of the rhyme-schemes has importance, since the tunes usually conform to them. Thirty-three varieties occur—3 for four-line stanzas, 5 for five-line, 8 for six-line, 2 for

[26]

A peculiar feature in about thirty cases is the use of a half-stanza at the end of poems with six or (more commonly) eight lines to the stanza. Psalm 18 begins and ends in this way. Every such case requires a tune that is correspondingly divisible.

Below is a complete tabular arrangement of the meters employed in the poetry:

TABLE I

CLASSIFICATION OF STANZA-PLANS OR METERS

		PSALMS	
Meters (by line syllables)		Marot	Beza
Four-line—	7 7 7 7*		136
	8 8 8 8		100=131=142 134
	8 8 9 9	9	
	9 8 8 9		141
	9 8 9 8	140=Dec	
	10 10 10 10		93
	10 11 10 11		129
	10 11 11 10		74=116
	11 10 10 11		87
	11 10 11 10	12 110	
	11 11 10 4	101	
	11 11 10 10	8	
Five-line—	8 8 8 8 8		132
	8 8 9 9 8	13	
	8 9 8 8 9	15	
	9 8 8 9 5	5=	=64
	9 9 8 8 9		96
	9 9 8 9 8	143	
	10 10 10 10 10		124
	10 10 11 10 11		57
	10 11 11 10 4	14=	=53

* Non-iambic.

seven-line, 8 for eight-line, 1 for nine-line, 4 for ten-line, and 2 for twelve-line. Three main types are to be marked—those coupling successive lines, those coupling alternate lines, and those where a couplet is *inset* within another that encloses it. "Pair-rhyme" and "cross-rhyme" are common in all languages, but "inset-rhyme" is much rarer. In modern English, the last is familiar from Tennyson's "In Memoriam." In the French Psalter this is evidently a favorite (as in Sidney, as might be expected). It is a curious fact, as Gosse tells us, that Tennyson actually supposed that he had *invented* this ancient scheme.

Two-thirds of the schemes are used by Marot, while but one-third were added by Beza.

TABLE I (*Continued*)

CLASSIFICATION OF STANZA-PLANS OR METERS

Meters (*by line syllables*)	Marot	Beza
Six-line— 5 6 5 5 5 6*		81
6 6 7 6 6 7	ND	
6 6 8 7 7 8		26
7 7 7 7 7 7*		75 135
8 4 7 8 4 7*	38	61
8 6 6 8 7 7		121
8 7 7 8 6 6		21
8 7 8 7 7 7*		146
8 8 8 8 8 8		117=127
8 8.8 8 9 9		30=76=139
8 8 9 8 8 9	113 24=	=62=95=111
8 8 9 8 9 8		106
8 8 9 9 9 9		83
8 9 9 8 9 9		88
9 6 6 9 7 7		31=71
9 6 6 9 9 5		125
9 6 9 6 8 6		52
9 7 6 7 7 6	6	
9 8 8 9 8 8		58
9 8 9 9 8 6	43	
9 9 8 8 8 8		80 94 105
9 9 9 8 8 9		55
9 9 9 9 8 8		28=109
9 9 9 9 9 9		112
10 8 10 8 10 8		39
10 10 7 10 10 7	114 115	
10 10 10 10 11 11		50
10 10 11 11 10 10	1	
10 11 10 11 10 11		119
10 11 10 11 11 11		16
11 10 11 10 11 10	37	
11 11 8 10 10 8		133
11 11 10 10 11 11	137	
11 11 10 11 11 10	103	
11 11 11 11 10 10		78=90
11 11 11 11 11 11	23	
12 12 13 13 13 13		89
Seven-line— 10 10 10 10 10 11 11	10	
11 10 11 10 11 10 11	11	

* Non-iambic.

TABLE I (*Continued*)

CLASSIFICATION OF STANZA-PLANS OR METERS

Meters (*by line syllables*)	Marot	Beza
Eight-line— 5 5 5 5 5 5 6 6*		99
6 8 8 6 6 8 8 6		34
7 6 6 7 7 6 6 7		92
7 6 7 6 6 7 6 7	107	
7 6 7 6 7 6 7 6	128 130	
7 7 7 7 8 7 7 8*		150
7 7 7 7 8 8 8 8*		29
8 7 8 7 7 7 8 8*		42
8 7 8 7 7 8 7 8*	25	
8 7 8 7 8 7 8 7	91	
8 8 7 7 8 8 7 7*	86=	=77
8 8 7 7 8 8 8 8*		102
8 8 8 8 9 9 8 8		126 148
8 8 8 8 8 8 9 9		60=108
8 8 9 8 8 9 8 8		84
8 8 9 9 8 8 8 8		35 73
8 9 9 8 8 9 9 8		54
8 9 9 8 9 8 8 9		17=63=70
9 6 9 6 9 6 9 6	72	
9 6 9 6 9 7 9 7		20
9 8 9 8 9 8 9 8	118=	=66=98
9 9 8 8 8 9 8 9		44
9 9 8 8 9 9 8 8	7 46=	=82 59
9 9 9 7 8 8 8 6		149
9 9 9 9 9 9 8 8		120
9 9 9 9 9 9 9 9		147
10 6 10 6 10 6 10 6		41
10 6 11 7 11 7 10 6		123
10 10 10 5 11 11 11 4	22	
10 10 10 7 11 11 11 6		56
10 10 10 10 10 10 10 10		85
10 10 10 10 10 10 11 11		49
10 10 10 10 11 11 11 11		145
10 10 11 11 10 10 11 11	104	
10 11 10 11 11 10 11 10	2	
10 11 11 10 10 11 10 11	51=	=69
11 10 11 10 10 10 10 10		27
11 11 10 10 11 11 10 10	32 45 18=	=144

* Non-iambic.

[29]

TABLE I (*Continued*)

CLASSIFICATION OF STANZA-PLANS OR METERS

Meters (*by line syllables*)	Marot	Beza
Nine-line— 6 6 7 7 6 6 6 6 6		97
Ten-line— 8 8 8 8 8 8 9 8 8 9		122
8 8 9 9 7 7 8 8 8 8*		48
9 8 9 8 6 6 5 6 6 5	33	
9 8 9 9 8 9 8 9 9 8	4	
10 8 8 10 7 7 6 6 6 6		40
11 11 11 11 6 6 7 6 6 7	79	
Twelve-line— 5 5 5 5 5 5 5 5 5 5 5 5*		47
6 6 6 6 6 6 6 7 6 6 7	19	
6 6 7 6 6 7 6 6 7 6 6 7	3	
8 4 5 8 4 5 8 4 5 8 4 5	138	
8 8 7 8 8 7 8-8 7 8 8 7	36=	=68

* Non-iambic.

It is easy to see that such meters call for melodies of no little length. One tune runs to 92 syllables and notes, another to 86, seven to 84, four to 82, two to 80, ten to 70 or more, while half of the tunes exceed 56 notes, which was the standard length in the earliest English tunes. Soon after 1600 British usage lapsed into using the "half" or "short" tune of 28 or 32 notes. To those wonted to this latter style the affluence of the French style is somewhat startling. Even today, when longer tunes have been revived, that the elaborate French melodies were once freely sung without book in myriads of homes, by workers in the field or shop, by travelers on the road, may well be counted incredible.[5]

Before leaving this topic of verse-forms, special mention is due to the notable poetic Psalter that was begun by Sir Philip Sidney before his lamentable death in 1586 and within a short period completed by his sister, the Duchess of Pembroke. This remarkable book was evidently inspired by Marot's example, as is shown by many similarities in both spirit and form. It was not framed for popular use in song, but simply as a piece of literary art. Its original circulation, though somewhat wide, seems to have been wholly in manuscript copies. So far as is known, it was not printed until revived in 1823 by the Chiswick Press. Probably only about forty versions are by

[5] See lines 41–47 of Marot's "Aux dames de France," prefixed to his *Cinquante pseaumes* (1543), as quoted in Douen, I, 397.

Sidney himself, but the dexterity of his sister almost equals his own felicity in diction and interpretation, so that the whole has a certain unity and sustained vigor.

Sidney, like Spenser, his contemporary and friend, was early familiar with the French genius for lyric poetry. In 1572, when on his first visit to the Continent, he witnessed the horror of St. Bartholomew in Paris, unharmed because he was the guest of Walsingham, the English envoy, who then and later strove to mitigate the enmity between the Catholic and Huguenot parties. It is possible that at this time Sidney acquired a copy of the Marot-Beza Psalter, issued ten years earlier.[6]

The Sidney meters number 125, besides some versions in irregular form. At least 25 are identical with those in French. Trochaic measures are used in 15 whole versions and partially in 12 others. Feminine endings occur often, though less so than in the French. Something of the style finds an echo in several works by George Wither between 1620 and 1640.

[6] Of course, the Sidneys used a style of expression that may be thought related to "euphuism." But the matter and spirit of their Psalter are far removed from the grotesque and empty affectation of the euphuists proper. The reason for emphasizing the Sidney book here is that it demonstrated on a large scale the entire capacity of Elizabethan poetry to match the variety and flexibility of French verse—just what the editors of the first English Psalter sought to avoid.

V

The Technical Character of the Tunes

W E TURN now to the melodies that were chosen to accompany the poetic texts.[1] In the completed French Psalter there were 125 tunes, besides about 30 others that had appeared in early editions, but were then discarded. As finally adjusted, 21 melodies were assigned to more than one poem. For purposes of study, they all need to be classified in a variety of ways, to be taken up in order.

But, to begin with, we must recall in outline the general situation of musical art and practice as it stood in the middle of the 16th century. The period was plainly one of transition. This may be partly attributed to the general influence of the Renaissance, or it may be traced rather to latent potencies within the art itself. However we regard these factors, it is clear that during this century the spirit and methods of the Middle Ages were being transformed into types that prefigured the music of the next three centuries. Between the old and the new there came to be decided differences. For a time there was more or less mingling of the two. The shift in style was not sudden and explosive, but a genetic development, not always moving with the same purpose or rapidity.[2]

In the mediæval period the formal pursuit of music was dominated by the tonal system known as "Gregorian." This system had been gradually evolved as an adjunct to ecclesiastical ritual, designed to provide melodies for the vocal declamation of prose texts, though somewhat extended to metrical poetry. Most of the melodies now

[1] From this point onward, and throughout Part II, the several tunes in the collection are referred to by the serial numbers of the Psalms with which they *first* appear in the completed Psalter, all mere repetitions of certain tunes being disregarded. Within each tune the successive lines or phrases are regularly designated by letters of the alphabet.

[2] The topic here briefly touched upon is discussed in all serious histories of music, though not with equal fullness or with entire agreement as to analysis and emphasis. The general view here expressed is more fully stated in the writer's *History of Music*, New York, latest ed. 1935, Part III.

extant are those coming from the Roman tradition. The total number may rise to several thousands.

This system rested upon a set of "modes" or "scales," doubtless derived from Greek prototypes, but having many features peculiar to itself. Its original object was to furnish guidance for cantillation in unison only. But before 1600 it had begun to expand into tonal fabrics of echoing and interlacing voices. Both the unisonal plainsong and the contrapuntal figured-song were intended for priestly ministrants or trained choristers only. After 1500 ecclesiastical polyphony was carried forward to a notable culmination by many composers, of whom Palestrina of Rome was so superior as to give name to the style as a whole.

Besides all this there was, far back in the mediæval period, another type of music, whose origin and aim were different. Almost every country and people in Europe came to have its own form of folk-music—songs and dances, usually with some slight instrumental accompaniment. The shaping of this style was not so much individual as communal, instinctive, and spontaneous rather than by rule or conscious reason. Most of it was long unrecorded, but handed on by rote. Yet its persistence was often remarkable and its prevailing qualities at length demanded recognition. It was in the 16th century that this manifold type of art began to have a decided effect upon the thought and practice of professional musicians. It proved to be potent enough to affect gradually the whole range of musical procedure. Its influence tended toward a new sense of tonal relation as expressed in modes or scales, toward basing structure more upon chords and harmonic sequences than upon melodic intervals and contrapuntal regulations, toward the expressive value of compact phrases and distinct sections in place of the continuous tapestry of interwoven melodic threads. It welcomed the use of solo as well as choral effects. It lifted instrumental writing into something like parity with that for voices alone. Its animating spirit was that of domestic and social warmth, energy, and humor rather than of churchly solemnity, and it tended toward emotional piquancies and intensities almost wanting in the older style. The quality of vivacity and infectious charm was often in evidence, especially in the Romance countries of Italy and France, where traditions of verse, song, and dance had become common as far back as the 12th century.

No statement like this of the collision of scholastic and popular styles of musical art during the 16th century can be adequate without discussing details that are out of place here. There was no organized warfare between them. But there was a complicated process of mutual interpenetration, out of which came a marked alteration in spirit and method, so that when the course of musical art crossed into the 17th century it was something different from what it had been a hundred years before.

It was during this transformation that the music of the Reformation was born and came first into wide-spread popular use. This music naturally reflected usages from both old and new styles. Yet, on the whole, it expressed tendencies that were new and revolutionary. Its total influence pointed forward rather than backward. That influence—considering the breadth and depth of its impact—may have been more of a factor in the results than has been usually recognized. In the French Psalter we have many features that show a close relationship with the Gregorian system, but they are combined with others that were not normal to that style. Some of these contrasted features must here be indicated in systematic outline.

Douen, in his great monograph to which we are constantly referring, makes it clear that he regards the tunes of the French Psalter as representing the transition of which we have been speaking.[3] He distributes the tunes into three classes as to mode, namely, (a) "la tonalité antique" (i.e., Gregorian), (b) "le mode mineur sans note sensible" (i.e., approaching the modern minor), and (c) "le mode majeur" (i.e., fully major).[4] To the first he assigns 52 tunes,

[3] See Douen, II, 337–42.

[4] Douen does not make plain what is meant by this "mineur," except that it is a transitional modality. Nor does he explain why he assigns certain tunes to this class. Further, he avoids the problem of "musica ficta." No one, however, can attribute these omissions to ignorance.

to the second 35, and to the third 38. Hence he concludes that a majority are more "modern" than strictly "antique." That any such classification is somewhat debatable is shown by his calling it a "résultat approximatif." His whole discussion of the matter is so thoughtful that it must be treated with respect, even when one is tempted to differ from it in details. Accordingly, we may well present it in tabular form. But, to increase its usefulness, it is important to classify the tunes in two other ways at the same time. The first addition is to distribute the tunes by their "finals" into five groups. The second is to place them also in three chronological groups. Concerning each of these extensions of Douen's statement it is necessary to offer some detailed explanation at this point, since it is convenient to use the same methods of presentation later.

1. For simplicity, the traditional list of modes is here reduced to five. These begin with the mode furthest from modern feeling and closes with that most characteristically modern. The series progresses systematically from one to the other, becoming steadily less marked by minor intervals (as counted from the "final"). Each mode may be used within either an "authentic" or a "plagal" range. Each, also, may be written either in its "natural" position or "transposed" (a fourth higher and using the tone B♭ instead of B).[5] The letter-names used do not indicate an absolute pitch, except that in any given mode or melody the relationship of tones is fixed with some exactness. Transferring the letters to the keyboard, as now tuned, does not precisely correspond in pitch to the practice of the olden time. The table of modes here used is as follows:

E-mode—	E	F		G	A	B	C		D	E
	1	2		3	4	5	6		7	8
A-mode—	A	B	C		D	E	F		G	A
	1	2	3		4	5	6		7	8
D-mode—	D	E	F		G	A	B	C		D
	1	2	3		4	5	6	7		8
G-mode—	G	A	B	C		D	E	F		G
	1	2	3	4		5	6	7		8
C-mode—	C	D	E	F		G	A	B	C
	1	2	3	4		5	6	7	8

[5] The condensed list of modes here used is not opposed to the traditional scheme. It is simply convenient in dealing with music that is modally somewhat mixed.

2. The date-groups represent the evident stages of editing through which the French Psalter passed. In the years between 1539 and 1551 some 80 tunes were tested out and 39 were finally retained, though not seldom slightly modified. In 1551 there were added 46 new tunes, and in 1562, 40 more.[6] During the first two periods the editor seems to have been Bourgeois, but in the final stage the editor was probably Pierre Dubuisson.[7]

TABLE II

THE TUNES AS CLASSIFIED BY DOUEN, ARRANGED BY MODE AND PERIOD

Tunes transposed are marked *

	Before 1551		*1551*		*1562*	
E-mode—			17	modal	83	modal
			26	.	94*	.
			31	.	102	.
			51	.	141	.
			100	.	147	.
			132	.		
A-mode—	4	minor	16	minor	55	modal
	6	.	39	.	106	.
	18	.	110	.		
	22	.				
	38	.				
	65	.				
D-mode—	5*	modal	28*	modal	48	modal
	13*	.	34	.	57*	.
	33	.	40*	.	59*	.
	50*	.	120*	.	80*	.
	104	.	125	.	146*	.
	114	.	7*	minor	148	.
	115	.	10	.	61*	minor
	128*	.	11*	.	88	.
	130*	.	12*	.	92*	.
	137	.	20*	.	96*	.
	143	.	37	.	112	.
	2*	minor	41*	.	149	.
	8	.	77	.		

[6] For details about the grouping of the tunes in three chronological sets, see Douen, I, 614–50.

[7] In the body of his work Douen refers to the final editor as unknown. But in one of his appendices (II, 633) he concedes the probability that it was Dubuisson.

TABLE II (*Continued*)

THE TUNES AS CLASSIFIED BY DOUEN, ARRANGED BY MODE AND PERIOD

Tunes transposed are marked *

	Before 1551		1551		1562	
	9	minor	129*	minor		
	14*	·				
	23*	·				
	24*	·				
	45*	·				
	77*	·				
	91	·				
	107*	·				
G-mode—	15	modal	30	modal	58	modal
	19	·	44	·	85	·
	103	·	46	·	87	·
			113	·	93	·
			117	·	136	·
			121	·	145	·
			126	·	74	major
			27	minor		
C-mode—	79	modal	3*	major	49	major
	1*	major	21*	·	52*	·
	32*	·	25*	·	54*	·
	36*	·	29*	·	56*	·
	43*	·	35*	·	60	·
	66	·	42	·	75*	·
	138*	·	47*	·	81	·
	140	·	73*	·	84*	·
	ND	·	101*	·	89	·
			119*	·	97*	·
			122*	·	99*	·
			123*	·	105*	·
			124	·	135*	·
			133*	·	150*	·
			134*	·		[8]

[8] In this table the distribution of tunes into chronological groups is highly important, indicating certain shifts of practice as the collection advanced from stage to stage.

Without challenging Douen's classification by modes in toto, the following examples may be cited as open to debate:

In the A-group, 16 and 39 may be modal, like 106.

In the G-group, 27 may be modal, while 15 is possibly major, like 74.

In the C-group, one wonders why 79 is not called major.

[37]

In this connection a word may be added about the difficulties in dealing with 16th-century melodies that arise from the possible use in them of the growing custom of *musica ficta*. This term commonly means the alteration of written or printed notes by a semitone to facilitate singing or to improve effectiveness. What are now called "accidentals" were as yet unknown or little used. Yet certain melodic alterations were becoming frequent.

The most imperative of these was to avoid the interval of the "tritone" (or augmented fourth) between two tones lying near together in a phrase. This usually involved reading the upper tone a semitone *lower* than as written.

Two other alterations were establishing themselves in the treatment of cadences. Where the melody approached the "final" from the tone below (especially by a "dipping" figure) the tendency was to read the penultimate tone a semitone *higher* than as written. With this went, wherever more than the bare melody was accompanied by other voices, a tendency to read the third in the final chord a semitone *higher* than as written—the so-called "tierce de Picardie." Both of these alterations were alien to the older Gregorian practice, and were steps away from its supremacy.

The absence of written or printed marks in music of this period makes it difficult to be sure just where these alterations were intended by the composer or introduced by the singer. As we pass into the 17th century such alterations—and many more—are duly marked. But in such cases we cannot be certain whether the usage indicated was that of the original or of the later period. As one compares scattered examples of the French Psalter from different centuries there is much disagreement in notation at certain points. It may be that it was because of this kind of uncertainty that Douen was cautious about entering in full the reasons for his classification.[9]

[9] As one collates later editions of the French Psalter, where accidentals become more and more numerous, he encounters applications of *musica ficta* that seem objectionable. Thus in the Dutch versions (from 1773 onward) many cases occur where the original melodies are strangely distorted.

VI

The Metric Patterns within the Lines

IN THE process of reducing the phenomena of the French tunes to systematic statement, we have now dealt with but two points, namely, (a) that the poetic texts are laid out in many meters, to which the tunes were naturally forced to conform, and (b) that the tunes themselves vibrate freely among various types of mode or scale. We now turn to a third point, equally important, but much harder to present briefly. This concerns the singular variety in the single lines as to the patterns of their long and short tones.[1] The lengths of the lines are fixed by the verse and its meters, but lines of the same length and accent are often given several different patterns in different tunes or even in the same tune. To some extent this may be due to outside sources, as where secular melodies are borrowed or closely imitated. But attentive study of the facts as a whole indicates that the collection is pervaded by some general tendency or intention to achieve large variety, while keeping to a certain general uniformity. Even more than the diversity of poetic meters or the use of all the accepted modes, this opulence in line-form goes far to constitute a particular "style" for the musical contents of the French Psalter. To it, therefore, we must give detailed attention.

In the Reformation songbooks generally, the lines or phrases are marked off by some kind of check-mark to aid singers in keeping their place. But within the lines the notes are not separated into measures by bars, though the "feet" of the verse give an implicit measure-form. We

---

[1] Here and elsewhere patterns of long and short tones are called "metric," because primarily determined by measuring or duration-relations. Many musicians, however, prefer to call such patterns "rhythmic"—a term more germane to accent-relations. The patterns remain significant phenomena, whatever adjective is applied. See discussions in the writer's *New Encyclopedia of Music and Musicians,* New York, rev. ed. 1929, under "Acoustics," "Meter," and "Rhythm."

may doubt whether originally the sense of "time" was always as rigid as in most modern music—certainly it was not strictly metronomic. Yet the rhythm was in mind, without being mechanical or obtrusive.

In general, only two forms of notes were used—breves and semibreves —with a longer note to mark the tune-end. We do not know whether, in actual singing, the values of the notes were made exact. We rather infer that they were kept flexible to the drift of the words and the contour of the phrase as a whole. We have no means of knowing whether the tempo was slow or fast. That in later times it became extremely slow seems certain. But we may be sure that the phrases were usually handled as separate units—not run together breathlessly, as so often in modern choir usage. Whether the accents were sharp and decisive is not clear. On this point we may remember that French poetry tends to be less emphatic than English.[2]

The total number of distinct patterns is over ninety, though some of these may seem like trifling variants. At least seventy-five are worth counting. Every one of these has its own effect of flow and accent, its own emotional content. Various features in the verse make for contrasted patterns—as where masculine and feminine endings are mingled, where part of a stanza is iambic and part trochaic, etc. Even among the fourteen tunes with equal lines, not one has the same pattern throughout (with possibly an exception in No. 47). In eleven tunes there is a different pattern for every line (including No. 123, which has eight lines). It is evident that in this respect the collection as a whole presents an aspect of remarkable freedom and diversity.

To present the data in systematic form for reference is impossible in musical notation. But, by using simple symbols, a compact list is worth making, with the number of occurrences in each period, as in Table III.

---

[2] It is not to be forgotten that these melodies were devised for unison singing without accompaniment and for singers fully wonted to such song both as music and as a vehicle for the inner import of the words. Such melodies have a large inherent freedom of movement and accent. Though far from being erratic or formless, many of them do not readily conform to the modern use of rigid measures and strictly recurrent accents. So not every modern singer catches the lilt and swing of these old-time tunes. Yet, when it is caught, it is eminently effective. The writer recalls many cases where, after a series of illustrations, most of the listeners were moved even to tears. No small part of this emotional impress is due to the varying pattern or figure of the phrases.

Metric Patterns

TABLE III

CLASSIFICATION OF LINE-PATTERNS,
WITH NUMBER OF CASES IN EACH PERIOD

Long and short notes are marked : and . respectively
Non-iambic patterns are indented

Line-length	Pattern	Early	1551	1562		Total	
4-note —	: . . :	2			=	2	
	: : : :	3	1			4	
	: . . :	2		2		4	
						—	
							10
5-note —	: . . : :	6	1		=	7	
	: : . . :		6	5		11	
	. . : : :			2		2	
	: . . . :		6	3		9	
	: . : . :	1				1	
						—	
							30
6-note —	: . . . . :	14	17	9	=	40	
	: . . : : :	24	13	7		44	
	: : : . . :		2			2	
	: . : : . :		2			2	
	: : . . : :	1		2		3	
	: . . . : :	3		2		5	
						—	
							96
7-note —	: . . . . : :	28	14	8	=	50	
	: : : . . : :	3				3	
	. . . : : : :		2			2	
	: : . . . . :	4	5	23		32	
	. . . . . . :			2		2	
	: : . . : : :	1	3	5		9	
	. : : : . . :			1		1	
	: . : . . . :		4			4	
	: . : . : : :		2			2	
	. . : . . : :	1				1	
	: : . : : . :			1		1	
						—	
							107

[41]

TABLE III (*Continued*)

CLASSIFICATION OF LINE-PATTERNS, WITH NUMBER OF CASES IN EACH PERIOD

Long and short notes are marked : and . respectively
Non-iambic patterns are indented

Line-length	Pattern	Early	1551	1562	Total
8-note —	: . . . . . . :	15	8	4	= 27
	: . . . . : : :	19	33	24	76
	: : : . . . . :		10	1	11
	: : : . . : : :	3	6	1	10
	: . . : : . . :	4	20	19	43
	: . . : : : : :	2			2
	: . . . : . : :			3	3
	: . . . . : . :		10	6	16
	. : : . . : . :	1			1
	. . : . . . . :			2	2
	: : : : . . : :	1			1
	: : . . . . : :	6	4	16	26
	: . : . . . : :		5		5
	: . . . : . : :	2	1		3
	: . . . : : : :	1	2	1	4
	: . : . . : . :		1		1
	: : . . . : . :		1		1
	: : . : . . . :		1	1	2

234

9-note —	: . . . . . . : :	15	21	26	= 63
	: : : . . . . : :	3	6	5	14
	: . . : : . . : :	12	13	29	54
	: . . : . : . : :	1			1
	: . : . : . . : :			1	1
	: . . . . . : . :	1	4		5
	: : : . . . . . :		3		3
	: . . : : . : . :	1			1
	: : . . : . . : :			1	1

142

10-note —	: . . . . :	2	1		3
	: . . . . . : : :	3	5	1	9
	: : : . . . . . :		2	2	4
	: : : : : . . : : :	5	1		6
	: : : : . . . . . :	5	1	1	7

TABLE III (*Continued*)

CLASSIFICATION OF LINE-PATTERNS,
WITH NUMBER OF CASES IN EACH PERIOD

Long and short notes are marked : and . respectively
Non-iambic patterns are indented

Line-length	Pattern	Early	1551	1562	Total
10-note —	: . . : : . . . . :	24	16	16	56
(*Cont.*)	: . . : : . . : : :	3	14	5	22
	: : : . . . . : : :	4	8	4	16
	: . . : : : . . : .	2			2
	: . . . : . : . : :			1	1
	: . . : : . : : . :		4	1	5
	: : : . . . : : . :		1	1	2
					—
					133
11-note —	: . . . . : :	5	6		11
	: . . . . . . : : :		1		1
	: : : . . . . . : :	1	7	2	10
	: : : : : . . . : :	5			5
	: . . : : . . . . :	36	20	13	69
	: . . : : . . : : :	1			1
	: : : . . . . : . :		1		1
	: . . : : . . . : :		2		2
					—
					100
12-note —	: . . : : . . . . . :	1	1		2
	: . . . . : : . . : : :			2	2
13-note —	: . . . . : : . . . . : :			3	3
	: . : : . : : . . . . : :			1	1
					—
					8
		277	318	265 =	860 [3]

The above list contains 76 forms of pattern. It is condensed from a fuller list of 92 by combining occasional cases where short notes occur at the beginning or end of lines instead of the more regular long notes.

As to rhythm, 24 appear to be non-iambic. As to line-endings, 28 are feminine, the others being masculine.

There is only one form (: : : :) with notes of even length throughout. All others have some mixture of longs and shorts.

[3] Technically, lines with an odd number of syllables and tones are usually feminine variants of those with an even number. Conceding this would result in reducing the total number in the above list by about a dozen.

Iambic forms regularly begin with one, three or five long notes, while non-iambic lines begin with two or four.

As a rule, short notes appear in groups of two, four, six or eight. In the midst of lines long notes usually appear in twos. Wherever this practice is varied, irregular forms occur, which require special comment.

There are 21 forms that are found in all of the three periods, covering 60 per cent of the total lines. Forms that are shared by the two periods number 19, leaving 36 that are found only in one period.

As Table III is arranged to show the freedom with which the French tunes deal metrically with lines of the same lengths, it implies more complication than really exists. Careful examination reveals that running through the whole are four principles of line-formation, two of which are more or less constant and primary, and two exceptional and secondary. In the two constant types, the short notes occur regularly in groups of two, four, six or eight, while in the two others they occur singly or in groups of three or (rarely) five. Long notes appear singly or in groups of from two to five.

The first and largest type of pattern is that in which lines begin and end with long notes, with two or more short notes in a chain in the middle. There are 35 patterns of this class, covering no less than 60 per cent of the total number of lines. The number of patterns of this kind is due partly to the frequency of feminine endings as well as masculine, and partly to the variety of groups in both long and short notes.

The second notable type of pattern is one in which the middle of lines is broken by two (or more) longs between groups of shorts. This occurs only in lines of eight notes or more, and tends to set up a median cæsura. There are 9 patterns of this class, covering about 30 per cent of the total number of lines. The use of this device is largely due to the abundant use of extended lines in French verse. This poetic trend has a notable effect on the music.

There remain over 30 patterns, covering only 10 per cent of the total number of lines. One part of these involves the use of triple feet instead of the prevailing duple—never carried through an entire tune, but involving interesting interminglings of triple and duple measures in single lines. The remainder comprises various syncopated effects at the ends of lines. In several cases these turn expected feminine endings into masculine. Both of these devices are somewhat peculiar to French usage, especially the second.

The lines in which these unusual effects occur are as follows:

	Early	*1551*	*1562*
Triple feet —			
	22*g*	25*f*	56*a*
	38*be*	29*cdh*	61*be*
	140*a*	42*abcdefgh*	141*abc*
		121*a*	148*a*
Syncopated endings —			
	6*a*	16*cf*	60*ad*
	43*bc*	20*a*	61*f*
		28*ad*	80*e*
		30*df*	85*c*
		31*a*	105*cd*
		34*ch*	145*c*
		35*a*	148*c*
		39*bd*	
		40*a*	
		41*c*	
		44*d*	
		73*a*	
		78*b*	
		100*a*	
		117*f*	
		120*b*	
		121*d*	
		122*g*	
		123*b*	
		124*c*	
		126*a*	
		129*ad*	

The syncopated effect also occurs in the first half of 89*f*, implying that the long poetic lines are musically conceived as each divided into two phrases.

The triplet effect is found usually in tunes that are non-iambic (trochaic). The syncopated effect is always in tunes that are iambic.

[45]

The comparative rarity of both effects in the early tunes is notable.[4] It is manifestly impracticable to present a full summary of the stanza-plans of all the tunes in this matter of varied patterns. But, as a concrete example, we may note the plans of the eleven tunes in which the pattern varies with every line:

Early		1551		1562	
8		30		87	
	: : : : : . . . . : :		: : : . . . . :		: : : . . . . . . : :
	: . . : : . . . . : :		: . . : : . . :		: . . : : . . . . :
	: . . : : . . : : :		: : : . . : : :		: : : . . : . . . . :
	. : : : : . . : : :		: . . . : : . :		: . . : : . . . . : :
9			: : : . . . . : :	92	
	: . . : : . . :		: : : . . . . : . :		: : : . . . . . . :
	: : : . . : : :	101			: : : . . . . : : :
	: . . . : : . . :		: . . . . : :		: . . : : . . . . :
	. : : . . . . : :		: . . . . : :		: . . : : . . : : :
13			: . . : : . . : : :		
	: . . . . :		: : : :		
	: . . . : . : :	121			
	: . . . . . . : :		: : . : . . . :		
	: . . : : . . : : :		: . . : : :		
	: . . : . . : :		. . . . . :		
43			: . . . : : . :		
	: : : . . . . : :		: . . . . : :		
	. : : . : : . :		. . . : : : :		
	: . . . . . . : . :	123			
	: . . : : . . : :		: : : . . . . : : :		
	: . . . . : : :		. . : . : . :		
	. . . . . :		: . . . . . . : : :		
			. . . : : : :		
			: . . . : : . . . . : :		
			. . . . . : :		
			: . . . : : . . : : :		
			. . . : : :		
		129			
			: . . . : : . : : . :		
			: . . : : . . . . : :		
			: . . : : . . : : :		
			: . . : : . . . : . :		

[4] Efforts have often been made to adjust the French patterns to barred notation as now used. Usually these tend toward more or less distortion of the melodies, even in books made by scholarly editors. In this respect even Gérold's *Clément Marot—Psaumes avec mélodies,* 1912, seems somewhat objectionable.

[46]

VII

Further Details of Line-Formation

THE ADEQUATE technical analysis of melodies is always difficult, since the subject presents so many facets. In the present investigation inquiry has been pushed in a large number of directions, both to gain a just sense of the French style and to facilitate comparison with cognate styles. The resulting data are not only highly technical, but intricate and voluminous, especially as they usually cover phenomena in the English and Scottish Psalters as well as those in the French.[1] From these data only a few points are here selected as illustrations.

(a) Identical lines. This phenomenon is common to all tune-literature. It appears in two distinct forms. The first is the repetition of lines or phrases within a given tune, so as to gain the artistic and practical value of direct duplication. These we shall call *repeats*. The second is the occurrence—whether deliberate or unconscious—of the same line in different tunes. These will be called *doublets*. In the French tunes, repeats are fairly common, especially in the early tunes and in the more frequent modes. They may be due in part to German influence. On the other hand, doublets are rather rare and most noticeable in the latest tunes.

TABLE IV

IDENTICAL LINES—REPEATS AND DOUBLETS

Repeats (within a given tune) —

	Early	*1551*	*1562*
A-mode —			
4	$e=f$		
65	$a=c$ $b=d$		

[1] In research of this kind lists must be made of all the instances in which a given form or effect appears, so that they can be enumerated and compared. Such lists vary greatly in practical value. Some prove to have but slight suggestion. Others reveal important points that cursory study does not disclose. In the present study, exhaustive lists of all sorts of phenomena have been in constant use. These cover not only the French tunes, but those original in the English and Scottish books—together amounting to about 1,600 lines.

TABLE IV (*Continued*)

IDENTICAL LINES—REPEATS AND DOUBLETS

Repeats (within a given tune)—

	Early	*1551*	*1562*
D-mode —			
	2 $a=c$ $e=g$	10 $a=c$ $b=d$	48 $a=b$ $c=d$ $g=h$
	33 $a=c$ $b=d$ $e=f$	37 $b=d$	80 $c=f$
	50 $c=d$	40 $e=f$ $h=i$	148 $e=f$
	77 $a=b$ $c=g$ $d=h$ $e=f$		149 $e=f$
	91 $a=c$ $b=d$		
	107 $a=c$ $d=h?$		
	143 $a=c?$ $b=d$		
G-mode —			
	19 $a=d$ $b=e=h$ $c=f$	27 $a=c$ $b=d$	
	103 $c=f$	46 $e=f$	
		113 $a=b?$	
C-mode —			
	1 $a=f$	25 $a=c$ $b=d$	60 $e=f$
	36 $a=d$ $b=e$ $c=f$ $g=h$	29 $e=f$	81 $a=c$ $d=e$
	66 $a=c$	42 $a=c$ $b=d$	89 $a=b$
	79 $e=f$	47 $f=l$	97 $e=f$
	138 $a=d$ $b=e$ $c=f$ $h=k$	122 $b=c$ $e=f$ $h=i$	105 $c=d$
			150 $a=b$ $f=g$

Note also that there were 26 cases in 13 tunes in the early period that were not finally retained.

Doublets (in different tunes) —

	Early	*1551*	*1562*
E-mode —			
			$83c = 147d$
D-mode —			
	107h =	= 20h = 40hi	
	114f =		= 149d
		41h =	= 149h
			61c = 146f
			80e = 148c
G-mode —			
		30c =	= 58d
		46c = 136g	

TABLE IV (*Continued*)

IDENTICAL LINES—REPEATS AND DOUBLETS

Doublets (in different tunes)—

	Early	*1551*	*1562*
C-mode —			
36*ad* = 138*j*			
36*l* = ND*f* =	= 123*d*		
		3*k* =	= 97*a*
		21*a* =	= 84*g*
		47*e* =	= 81*ac*
		47*g* =	= 81*de*
		133*c* =	= 105*f*
			75*e* = 135*e*
			84*de* = 105*cd*
			135*e* = 150*ab*

(b) Division into Tune-Sections. All the early Reformation tune-writing tended to divide the longer melodies into two contrasted sections, usually equal in length or nearly so. As a rule, both sections close with the "final" of the mode. In the French tunes such a division was obligatory in about 30 cases, due to the occurrence of half-stanzas in the verse (see Chapter IV). But it is also part of the general movement toward balanced "form" in the modern sense. The comparative formlessness of plain-song was undergoing a reordering under the influence of secular song and dance. The adoption of metrical verse, with its equal or commensurate lines, its rhyming couplets and the like, and its reiterating stanzas, was matched in many ways in the disposition of the melodies as well. These were not only laid out in compact wholes to fit the stanzas, but marked off into sections and even smaller divisions. And musical rhyme appears in several different forms, not only in line-endings, but in line-openings, sometimes in exact duplication, sometimes in ingenious imitation. Of these formulating devices the French tunes are full of examples.

One special way of marking the transition from the first section to the second is by an octave-leap from the last note of the one to

[49]

the first note of the other. This striking effect, which may be of German derivation, is also occasionally used simply to set apart lines rather than sections. The instances are found in the following tunes:

(Early) 2, 19 (twice), 23, 32, 36, 91, 104, 107, 138.
(1551) 10, 27, 35, 37, 40, 122.
(1562) 49, 112, 148.

(c) Range or Ambitus. The compass of the tunes taken as wholes, is normally an octave (91 tunes out of 125), but may be a ninth (20 tunes) or a seventh (7 tunes). The remaining tunes (4, 15, 38, 74, 102, 141) have a compass of only a sixth.

The compass of single lines varies considerably. Out of a total of 862, the large majority (84 per cent) range from a fourth to either a fifth or a sixth, while 74 lines rise to a seventh, and 50 lines to an octave, and 12 lines fall to a third (31c, 33ef, 41b, 47fk, 61e, 77ef, 79g, 99cd). The relatively large number with a range of a seventh or an octave is plainly connected with the frequency of long lines, which give room for sweeping melodies.

Among the octave-lines, three-quarters lie in the D- or C-modes, all ranging either from 1 to 8 or from 5 to 5. But those in the E-mode range from 6 to 6, those in the A-mode from 3 to 3, and most of those in the G-mode from 4 to 4.

It is a curious fact that while the octave-lines usually show much freedom of melodic construction, the seventh-lines tend to run into mere diatonic scale-figures.

In this connection we may note that more than half of the tunes begin with tone 1 of the mode (72 tunes out of 125, including five that open with tone 8). The remaining 53 tunes begin mostly with tone 5 (42 tunes) or with tone 3 (10 tunes).

It is noticeable that the proportion of tunes *not* beginning with tone 1 increases steadily by periods—31 per cent early, 50 per cent in 1551, 60 per cent in 1562.

(d) Melodic Motion. In every melodic phrase the advance from tone to tone may take either of three courses. It may be *chantwise*

[50]

(to a tone on the same degree), *stepwise* (to a tone one degree above or below), or *skipwise* (to a tone more than one degree above or below). The first two motions are called diatonic or conjunct and the third disjunct. The contour and effect of the phrase as a whole is largely fixed by the choice and mingling of these motions. Thus the character of whole tunes, being made up of a certain number of phrases, depends much upon their similarity or contrast in formation or figure. For a full estimate other points are important, but the phenomena of melodic action demand attention by themselves.

In all early Protestant tunes diatonic motions decidedly predominate. In the French tunes they average about 80 per cent. One tune (No. 81) is wholly diatonic. Out of 862 lines, 180 (21 per cent) are also wholly diatonic, and all others partly so. Without taking space for the percentages of diatonics and skips for all the tunes, we may simply note those tunes that depart most from the average, as follows:

EXAMPLES OF THE VARYING BALANCE BETWEEN
DIATONIC STEPS AND SKIPS

Diatonics high—Skips low—

		Early	1551	1562
100%	0%			81
94	6		20	
			121	
93	7		124	
92	8	77	42	
		140		
91	9	5	10	
		43	117	
90	10	114		
89	11	19	30	
			31	
			37	
			110	
88	12	18	119	60
		32		
		65		
		103		
87	13		47	48

Diatonics low—Skips high—

		Early	*1551*	*1562*
74%	26%	2		87
		104		96
				150
73	27	107	25	94
72	28		126	88
71	29	91	16	
			100	
			132	
70	30	9	113	97
				106
				141
				147
69	31			146
66	34	8		
65	35			59
62	38		78	
61	39	12		80

Note the contrasts between periods.

A list of the percentages of diatonic intervals relative to tune-lengths shows that the tunes arrange themselves in three grades, those above 85 per cent diatonic, those between 75 per cent and 85 per cent, and those 75 per cent or lower, as follows:

	Early	*1551*	*1562*		
I.	10	15	5	=	30
II.	23	12	18		60
III.	6	12	17		35

The extremes are marked by No. 81 (100 per cent) and Nos. 12 and 80 (only 61 per cent).

About two-thirds of the 1,250 skips occur singly. The rest occur mostly in connected pairs or in threes or even fours. In addition, there are many cases where pairs of skips are separated by a single diatonic step or even by two such steps. Thus are set up what may be called "skip-figures." All told, there are about 80 such figures.

Of these, those that make a melodic "peak" (up-down motion) or a melodic "dip" (down-up motion) are specially noticeable—the dips much outnumbering the peaks. The statistics cannot well be presented here.

About one-third of the lines begin with a skip and a small number end with a skip. In each case there is some evidence of progress by periods, but in reverse directions, as the following figures show:

Lines with opening skips—

	Early	1551	1562		
Thirds up	42	43	50	=	135
" down	10	22	24	=	56
Fourths up	9	11	25		45
" down	4	1	3		8
Fifths up	17	22	4		43
" down	2	0	3		5

$$223 + 69$$

Lines with closing skips—

Thirds down	7	7	1	15
Fourths down	2	4	0	6
Fifths up	1			1
" down	2	2	1	5

$$1 + 26$$

(e) Recurrent Melodic Figures. In the French tunes, as in analogous collections, certain forms of melodic expression appear more or less often, reminding one of the idioms and favorite verbal phrases of speech. Most striking of these are the various formulæ that recur constantly at the opening or closing of lines or phrases. Many others may be noted within the middle of lines. Some cases are peculiar to this or that mode. Others are imitated more or less closely from mode to mode. Some seem rather peculiar to the French style. Others are common in other styles. It is hopeless here to mention more than a sample or two out of the extensive lists that might be given.

[53]

Details of Line-Formation

The most salient figure among the line-openings is a triple repetition of the same tone, forming a sort of musical dactyl at the head of iambic lines. With this we are familiar as the opening of Luther's famous melody for "Ein' feste Burg." This device is chiefly found in the early French tunes, steadily decreasing in the later ones. It is likely due in some way to German influence, though not conspicuous in German melodies of the same period. The list of cases is as follows:

TRIPLE MONOTONE OPENINGS

E-mode —	4th tone (of mode)		51e	
A-mode —	1st tone	6a		
	3rd "	4a	16c	
		4i	39b	
	5th "	4cf		
		4h		
		22e		
		22f		
		65ac		
D-mode —	lower 5th		40a	
	1st tone	9a	37a	
		13a		
		23a		
		104f		
		114a		
	3rd "	24d	20b	
			40hi	
			120e	
	5th "	5c	34b	92a
		23c	125e	92c
		50cd		
		104h		
		114d		
	8th "	2eg	37bf	96a
		5b		
		8b		
		14a		
		104e		
		143bd		

TRIPLE MONOTONE OPENINGS (*Continued*)

G-mode —	1st tone	15*a*		85*a*	
				93*d*	
	2nd "	15*c*			
	4th "		44*h*		
	5th "		46*a*		
	8th "	19*g*			
C-mode —	2nd tone	43*d*			
	3rd "	43*c*	134*b*	49*c*	
		79*g*		56*g*	
	5th "	32*f*	3*i*		
		32*g*			
	8th "	32*e*			
		36*gh*			
	Tunes	23	13	5 = 41	
	Cases	41	17	7 = 65	

Among the figures found in line-ends it is enough to cite the syncopated one already described in Chap. VI, the list of cases there given being unnecessary to repeat. One feature of this, however, requires mention here. The syncopated effect occurs in all the modes, but is almost wholly confined to tunes in 1551 and 1562. In all cases it closes with a "dipping" figure, in its characteristic form using a short note rising by a semitone to the "final." Yet it also appears with a close on tone 5 of the scale, and even with tones 4, 3, and even 2 and 7. How far the semitone close is to be admitted is not certain, though the analogy of many endings that are *not* syncopated suggests its possibility. It is to be remembered that line-endings in upward motion are decidedly infrequent throughout the French tunes. When they occur, they usually arrest attention, since often they imply a leaning toward modern types of cadence.

French usage much prefers ending lines with a downward step instead of an upward—the ratio being about two to one, or, if certain cases be disregarded as incidental, perhaps as high as nine to one.

A special interest attaches to the question of contour in the lines taken as wholes. In the French tunes this feature acquires special importance because of the large proportion of long lines, which give room for considerable melodic evolution. Study of this matter is facilitated by making diagrams or graphs of many lines for comparison.

There is a marked tendency toward a pointed or arched contour, rising to one or more peaks and then descending to a cadence. The favorite form has two peaks (58 per cent), but one peak only is common (22 per cent) and, per contra, three or even four peaks (21 per cent). The last group tends away from the arched form toward a contour that is serrate or wavy (in 23*d,* for instance, dropping to a mere ripple). The number of lines with the reverse contour (with a valley shape) is notably small, though dips in the middle are frequent, without controlling the contour as a whole.

VIII

The Importance of the 1551 Edition

IN ANY thoughtful survey of the gradual evolution of the French Psalter between 1539 and 1562 one can hardly fail to see that the edition of 1551–54 occupies a pivotal position. It was then that the compilation of both verse and music passed out of its tentative or experimental stage into its first permanent maturity. It was not till then that a majority of the Psalms had been translated into verse, giving it the right to be called a "Psalter" and not merely a fragment. On the side of the tunes, also, there are many details of practice and style which then mark something more than a mere step forward. What was then decided upon became fixed and authoritative. Just at this point, it may be incidentally noted, the British Psalters took up their rather rapid development, soon becoming independent to a greater or less degree. We may be unable to discern exactly why all these things came to pass. But the facts invite discussion.

As regards the tunes, the 1551 edition retained 39 out of the 80 that had been tested during the preceding twelve years. The texts for these were all by Marot. There were now added 46 more tunes, making 85 in all. Of these additions, 12 were fresh settings of poems by Marot and 34 were adapted to altogether new poems by Beza, the numbers of the tunes being as follows:

To words by Marot—

    3, 7, 10, 11, 12, 25, 37, 46, 51, 101, 110, 113.

To words by Beza—

    16, 17, 20, 21, 26, 27, 28, 29, 30, 31, 34, 35, 39, 40, 41, 42, 44, 47, 73, 78 (90), 119, 120, 121, 122, 123, 124, 125, 126, 117 (127), 129, 131 (100), 132, 133, 134.

From these figures it is evident that in 1551 strikingly new elements in the contents of the collection now made their appearance.

In the tunes brought over from the early period 35 distinct meters appear in 1551, while in the new tunes 41 other meters are added, making 76 meters for 85 tunes. Beza's evident avoidance of the exact meters used by Marot seems to be deliberate, though the general style of structure remains the same. It is to be noted that in his later poems Beza changed his method slightly—on the one hand copying from Marot somewhat more, and on the other tending to employ rather more non-iambic forms.

In 1551 two shifts in meter set in, both of which were continued in 1562, namely,

(a) more non-iambic measures—
    Early— 2½ tunes (20 lines)
    In 1551—4   tunes (26 ")
    In 1562—9½ tunes (64 ")
(b) more 4-, 6- and 8-line stanzas—
    Early— 73% of the lines
    In 1551—83% "
    In 1562—90% "

During the early period, though all the modes had been used, the E-mode was finally discarded. In 1551 and again in 1562 this mode reappears in 11 tunes in all. Just why Bourgeois turned away from this noble mode in 1542 and 1549 and returned to it in 1551 is not clear. It may be that there was some change in the conditions under which he was working. For details, see Table II, p. 36.[1]

Associated with this shift in modal balance is a notable increase in the use of the plagal form of modes instead of the authentic. In the early tunes the proportion of plagal ranges is only 23 per cent, while in 1551 it is 46 per cent and in 1562, 30 per cent.

Various points in line-structure that have been noted in previous pages need to be recalled here as emphasizing the change of method that set in with 1551. The most striking are these:

---

[1] The two E-mode tunes used before 1551 were both from Strassburg, one from the 1539 book, the other from the Pseudo-Roman (1542). The first (for Ps. 91) continued until 1549, though somewhat altered. In 1551 it was replaced by a new tune, in the D-mode. But the older tune was kept in mind, though the general effect was different. The second tune (originally for Pss. 4 and 13) was replaced within a year by another in the D-mode. Here, again, there are traces of the Strassburg melody.

(a) The device of "repeats" is characteristic of the early period—35 cases in 16 tunes before 1551, 19 cases in 12 tunes in 1551, 14 cases in 10 tunes in 1562.

(b) In the matter of "doublets" the reverse is true—the later tunes showing more than the earlier.

(c) There is a steady increase in the practice of beginning melodies with some other tone than the first of the mode—31 per cent in the early tunes, 50 per cent in 1551, 60 per cent in 1562.

(d) The device of a three-note monotone opening is clearly early—42 cases before 1551, 15 in 1551, 7 in 1562. Similar changes might be adduced regarding other formulæ of opening and closing.

(e) The relative amount of diatonic steps decreases steadily, but by no great amount.

(f) As to the use of metric patterns in the lines, if we exclude those that are common to three periods, it appears that 21 occur only in early tunes (40 lines), while 40 are confined to later tunes (137 lines).

Such data as those that have been indicated raise a problem about which there is little external evidence. This problem concerns not only the identity of the musical editor or editors, but also the influences that probably affected the editorial process. Douen's contention seems plausible that for all the official editions from late in 1542 till 1557 Louis Bourgeois was the chief, if not the only, musical supervisor. Yet, even so, we gather that the position which he held was never quite what it would be today. He was but one wheel in a somewhat complicated system. The mainspring and governor in this system was certainly Calvin. Under him were the two poets who were charged with supplying the versified texts. Decidedly subordinate was the musician who collected, arranged, or composed the melodies that really gave vitality and endurance to the total result. All these, moreover, were technically subject to the legal authority of the City Council at Geneva—though this latter only rarely becomes important.

The problem revolves mainly about the four men most actively concerned. These, in order of age, were Marot, born (probably) in 1497, who, if he had lived till 1551, would have been fifty-four; Calvin, born in 1509, who in 1551 was forty-two; Bourgeois, born about 1510 and therefore also over forty; and Beza, born in 1519 and so just past thirty.

As to Marot: In 1551 he had been dead seven years, so that he had no direct connection with the edition of that year. But, since in that edition nearly half of the tunes included originated before he died, his indirect influence may have been considerable. Some notes are therefore in order concerning what may have been the nature of that influence.[2]

So far as we know, Marot's musical interest was rather popular or secular than ecclesiastical. Apparently, his original impetus was wholly literary, though coupled with musical aptitude. For his first sheaf of translations we are told that existing melodies were used. Possibly he added melodies of his own, especially as he was working with somewhat uncommon verse-forms. It is not clear, however, that any of these casual melodies entered into the standard list of Psalter tunes. With the 1539 and 1542 Strassburg books and with their partial adoption at Geneva Marot had nothing to do. But from late in 1542 he was at Geneva and soon engaged in making additional texts for Calvin. It is fair to conjecture that then, because he was older than either Calvin or Bourgeois and held a place as a recognized poet, he may have had some influence upon the selection of tunes to go with his poems. If so, its effect may have continued after his departure and death. About all this we have no real knowledge. At the best it is not likely to signify much.

As to Calvin: We have already noted how early he committed himself to the promotion of psalmody as a feature of church and domestic life. Though defeated in his initial effort in this direction

---

[2] The Marot family first appears near Caen in Normandy, but the name was then Marais, de Mares, Desmarets, or the like. The form "Marot" was assumed by Jehan, Clément Marot's father. Jehan was long in service as secretary to the forceful Anne of Brittany (twice Queen of France), and then (1515–26) valet de chambre to Francis I. He was well known as a fair poet, as shown by various editions of his works. Why his son Clément was born at Cahors (in south central France) is not clear. Properly the family was Norman or Breton. Thence it is traceable into Flanders.

Among the Huguenot settlers in America are names like Marais, Demarest, and Marot. Where the latter form is preserved today the descent is supposed to have come through Clément's son, Michel. See Douen, I, 36.

at Geneva, during his four years at Strassburg as leader in the first French Protestant church, he doubtless had connection with the small 1539 book, to which many think he contributed metrical versions of his own, and may have assisted in the compilation of the tunes, though the latter seems more likely to have been in Greiter's hands.

When, in 1542, Calvin was recalled to Geneva and seated there in his lifelong position of dominance, he promptly adopted all of Marot's first thirty translations in their authentic form and enlisted the poet as a co-worker in expanding their number. His loyalty to the quality of Marot's work remained unbroken to the end, though Marot died twenty years before Calvin—and this in spite of whatever in Marot's personality or actions may have offended Calvin's strict ideas. The same steadfast support seems to have been given by Calvin to the much humbler Bourgeois throughout the fifteen years of the latter's work at Geneva. Just before 1551 the City Council actually put Bourgeois in jail for having modified certain tunes without their permission. It was Calvin who had him set free at once. And it is significant that in the 1551 book the tunes appear as Bourgeois modified them. Yet it is not known that Calvin had any specific expertness in musical technique.

Undue emphasis has sometimes been placed on Calvin's refusal to have the Psalter tunes printed with harmony. His attitude may not mean more than that such printing would much increase the bulk and expense of the Psalm-books, or that he doubted whether harmonic practice had become sufficiently settled before the middle of the century.

As to Bourgeois: The dates of his birth and death are unknown, as are almost all details of his life in Paris before 1541 and after 1557. His call to Geneva came from the City Council and not from Calvin (who was then not there). At first he was associated with Guillaume Franc, who however removed to Lausanne in 1545, where he worked out an independent set of Psalm-tunes (never widely used). Bourgeois succeeded to Franc's office as choirmaster at St. Pierre in

[61]

Geneva, for a time assisted by one Fabri. His special work was as singing-master in a school and at the Cathedral, but, under Calvin's patronage, he became established as the musical editor of successive editions of the Psalter until 1557. In 1547 at Lyons he issued twenty-four of the Psalm-tunes in harmony (besides some original tunes), and as late as 1561 further harmonizations of all the tunes then in use. In addition, in 1550 he put forth a textbook in singing, in which he empasized an improved system of solmization. There is no sign that he had any part in the final edition of the Psalter, save that all his tunes, as in the 1551 book, were there incorporated in full, and that the final editor clearly sought to conform, as far as he was able, to Bourgeois' general style.

During his early editorship he discarded nearly forty tunes (including some presumably his own). Excluding those that are traceable to Strassburg, there remain at least seventy that constitute his permanent monument. How far these may have been derived by him from external sources and how many were in some sense composed by him is a difficult question about which one must be cautious. That he made use of many first lines of secular chansons, followed by an independent development, is evident—this use of well-known "motto-lines" being a common practice of the time. Through all his work, as finally settled, runs a sureness of touch and a degree of freedom that imply that he was a serious and skillful artist. To him is plainly due the individual style that sets the French Psalter apart from all others of its age. Yet, having said all this, we still do not see a full reason for the differences of the 1551 edition from its predecessors.[3]

As to Beza: Between Marot and Beza there were some points of likeness, but more of difference. Both early displayed gifts of energy and the promise of personal power, though in different spheres.

---

[3] Just why Bourgeois left Geneva for Paris in 1557 is not known. His interest in the Reform had certainly not ceased. During the next five years the Psalter on which he had worked was finally brought to completion. In the body of Douen's treatise the final editor is spoken of as unknown. But in Appendix III to the second volume Douen adopts the plausible view that the musical editor was a certain "Pierre," who was then choirmaster at Geneva—probably Pierre Dubuisson, a musician otherwise almost unknown.

Both had evident literary ability, Marot inheriting from his father poetic aptitudes that soon raised him to eminence, while Beza, after some efforts in verse-making, turned rather into the path of scholarship. Both had legal training, whence Marot gained only mental discipline and a sense of men and affairs, while Beza, after winning his degree in 1539, engaged in practice in Paris.

But the two men were variously unlike. They were born into distinct grades of society. Marot was of the middle class, always (like his father) dependent for support upon the favor of royalty and socially welcome only for his wit and bonhomie. Beza, on the other hand, belonged to the minor nobility, possessed several sources of income, and had entrée into high society.[4] By way of formal education, Marot had little regular schooling, though disciplined through manifold experiences, ranging from active service in military operations to more than one imprisonment for the freedom of his tongue and pen, while Beza spent at least ten years in the then famous universities of Orléans and Bourges. Thus the latter came under the intimate guidance of the eminent Greek scholar Wolmar (earlier also Calvin's teacher), receiving not only impetus toward linguistic studies, but also sound information about the growing movement in the direction of ecclesiastical reconstruction. Marot's spiritual awakening was gradual, erratic, and more mystical than logical. Beza's was sudden, in the midst of a severe illness, and issued in immediate action. He then turned his back upon the gay life of Paris and betook himself to Geneva. There he speedily stood forth as Calvin's most energetic and capable assistant. Thus he brought to the Reform a notable accretion of high-born culture, eminent enthusiasm and diplomatic skill.

As Beza had had some training for the priesthood, he doubtless had intimate knowledge of Catholic music as then practiced. His years in Parisian society must have made him familiar, also, with

[4] Beza (latinized for de Besze) was of Burgundian descent, born at Vézelay, where his father was castle-governor. His education was largely supervised by his uncle, a prominent lawyer in Paris. His Parisian life was not without moral blemish. But his conversion was complete and lasting. Apart from his Psalm-translations his writings lie wholly in the realm of exegesis and theology. See Douen, I, 547 ff. and article in Schaff-Herzog, *op. cit.*

much secular music. As music was then fashionable, he naturally dabbled in it as an accomplishment. In his later life we know that he essayed sundry melodies for Psalms and cantiques.[5] So we have every right to assume that in making his long chain of Psalm-versions from about 1550 he gave due heed to the tunes to which they were to be sung. Working in a small city like Geneva, he must have been in constant touch with both Calvin and Bourgeois. In such consultation he stood in a place of authority higher than that of Marot, even though he was much younger. Whatever preferences he may have had as to the musical details are likely to have had influence.

In view of these points, any fair study of the peculiarities of the 1551 edition must allow for the possibility—even the probability— that some of them are traceable to Beza. In just what direction his influence was thrown we can only conjecture. He may have simply secured for Bourgeois full freedom and assurance to work out his own ideals. It may be that Beza's views brought about some change in the balance of those of Bourgeois. It may be that the two men were somewhat opposed, in which case the wishes of the poet and embryo leader were likely to have prevailed. The present writer inclines toward assuming the first of these three alternatives.

[5] For examples, see Douen, I, 644–47.

IX

Polyphonic Settings of the Melodies

SINCE in all the early Protestant tune-books the melodies were regularly printed without other voice-parts, it is often supposed that nothing but unison singing was intended or practiced. It is true that Calvin opposed the printing of harmonized versions, partly because he felt that they would distract attention from the sense of the words, partly, perhaps, for other practical reasons. Doubtless in many gatherings for worship no other method was possible. In France there were many times and places where all Psalm-singing was hushed through fear of hostile attack.

But, on the other hand, we cannot overlook the notable fact that in Germany, France, and England harmonized or even contrapuntal versions followed close upon the first melodic versions. The earliest in France was Bourgeois' setting of Marot's "Fifty Psalms" for four voices, which was published at Lyons in 1547. About fifteen years later (1561) he issued at Paris settings of eighty-three Psalms by Marot and Beza for four, five, or six voices. Neither of these, however, found great acceptance.

During the latter half of the century we encounter several more significant and influential versions in varied forms by nearly a score of composers. Among these, the most admired are those by the experienced Claude Goudimel, who was earlier known by secular chansons and by masses for the Catholic service. From as early as 1551 he issued arrangements of the Huguenot tunes in motet style, and in 1565 set the whole Psalter in simple note-for-note harmony. This latter collection, after his violent death in 1572 (as one of the St. Bartholomew victims), was reissued again and again in France and other countries, even until the 19th century, because fitted for congregational use. Probably next to Goudimel in popularity was

Claudin Le Jeune, whose settings also ranged from the elaborately polyphonic to the simply harmonic—the latter attaining wide and prolonged circulation. Other early French composers to discourse in counterpoint upon melodies drawn from the Huguenot Psalter were Jannequin and Jambe-de-Fer. Even the eminent Orlandus Lassus, then in Munich, chose Huguenot tunes for themes in 1575–78, and, still more, the great Dutch organist, Jan Sweelinck, at Amsterdam in 1612–14.

Since these melodies were widely known in Holland and Germany throughout the 17th century, it is probable that, as the practice of polyphony shifted from the mystic restraint of the Palestrina school toward the daring freedom of the Bachs, they often supplied "subjects" for works that are now little known. In the early 18th century, it is to be noted that Johann Sebastian Bach chose as the theme of one of his Choralvorspiele the Alsatian song which in the French Psalter was first used for Ps. 36 and later made famous as the "Battle Song" in the Huguenot wars (1562–72); later still it was elaborated into the gigantic chorus which closes the first division of Bach's St. Matthew Passion (1729)—thus unconsciously celebrating the two hundredth anniversary of the melody's origin. Cases of like reminiscence are even noted in the 19th century, as in Schumann and Mendelssohn. There are probably many more.

Douen, in his second volume, devotes much space to this topic, with special notices of Certon, Bourgeois, Louis, Jannequin, Champion, Jambe-de-Fer, Goudimel, Crassot, Sureau, Servin, Santerre, Ferrier, Lassus, Lestocart, Le Jeune, Mareschall, Sweelinck, Stobäus and Crüger, followed by about 230 pages of examples *in extenso*.

It goes without saying that in touching upon this subject, which, of course, is here incidental, we are confronted with large historical questions about which opinions differ. That the 16th-century approach to composition was not that of today is evident. But how the two are to be related is not so clear. The contrast between the instinct of the first framers of congregational song and of those who expanded this song into artistic elaboration, on the one hand, and that of the present age of complication and even of innovating experiment, on the other, is certainly great. The critical question is whether we are to regard the present view as genetically evolved from that of four centuries ago or as intrinsically alien and hostile. To the present writer it seems that following down the history of the small form of the "tune" leads inevitably to the first attitude rather than to the second—the very smallness of the form facilitating analysis and amplification.

Historical truth and justice require that, first of all, such melodies as those of the French Psalter shall be viewed in the atmosphere of their own day, with the harmonic and contrapuntal treatments that were then made. But, at the same time, one may be permitted also to consider them as at many points prefiguring and preparing the way for other treatments, of which the 16th century had only dim and misty conception. The harmonies of Goudimel, for example, need to be borne in mind as they are. But other harmonies are possible that are germane to the latent quality of the melodies. So with contrapuntal elaboration. But the naïve and heartfelt directness and vigor of the original must not be allowed to escape or be distorted.

X

Early Diffusion of the French Tunes Outside of France

IT SEEMS almost paradoxical that the practical influence of the French tunes was largely achieved outside of France. This was due to the fact that Calvin's type of doctrine and polity promptly became powerful in many lands. This type included a plan of worship in which Psalm-singing was a prominent feature. The diffusion of this practice of combined poetry and music, which was in a sense incidental, seems to have been fostered and accelerated for its own sake. Whether the popularity of the French style was due primarily to the quality of its verse or to the variety of its music cannot be determined. The poetic and the tonal factors were inextricably woven together by the metrical form and the artistic purpose which they shared in common. That in so many cases the words were literally translated into languages that were decidedly alien to French is more surprising than that the tunes so generally went with them. No comprehensive survey of this subject will be attempted here. But two or three instances deserve mention in some detail.

The most important example is that of Holland. In the 16th century this northern part of the Low Countries was already notable, though not fully unified or politically independent. The strangling hold of Spain was broken but slowly and at the cost of much blood. Yet by 1574 the incipient Dutch nation began to be officially affiliated with Calvinism, by 1581 asserted its claim to be a sovereign state, by 1602 set about vast projects in the Far East that grew into its present colonial empire there, and by 1609 had planted settlements on the shores of America. The Dutch instinct for manufacture and maritime commerce was making Holland one of the richest and most powerful nations of Europe. Though racially

Teutonic, by religion it became linked with French Huguenotism and when the latter was extinguished in 1685 the Dutch people stood to a certain degree in the place of an heir, especially as large numbers of the expelled Huguenots fled to Holland for refuge—just as, a century earlier, the persecuted English Separatists had done.

Within four years of the completion of the French Psalter it was adopted as the song-manual of the Reformed Church of the Netherlands, though at first burdened with an inferior translation of the words. Thus it has ever since been maintained, though somewhat modified and much extended. The Dutch-French Psalter is still a living force, not only in Holland itself, but also in its distant colonies. The total Dutch circulation of the French tunes—extending through more than three centuries—probably much exceeds that within the original Huguenot domain.[1]

The second important diffusion of the French tunes took place in Germany. At the outset of the Reformation there was much interchange of sympathy between various leaders and groups that ultimately became separate, and, even in the land of Luther, when Calvin appeared portions of the latter's system commanded attention and imitation. The bewildering partition of German states favored the growth of diverse opinions and practices almost side by side. The influence of Geneva early extended northward as well as westward, into the Palatinate, Hesse and beyond. Though never equal in numbers or influence to the state church (Lutheran), yet the German Reformed Church grew steadily in significance through the 17th and 18th centuries. Since 1817 the two bodies have been united in the Evangelical Church. It was for the Reformed churches that the German translation of the French Psalter was

[1] No attempt is here made to make reference to the whole development of psalmody in Holland or its literature, some of the examples of which have been consulted. We may note that very early another translation of the French Psalter was made by Uitenhove, also using the French meters and melodies. Its influence, however, was less than that of Datheen.

From 1814 the drafting of versions in various languages in Asia and Africa was stimulated by sundry missionary enterprises. See Julian, *op. cit.*, article "Dutch Hymnody"; also notes 6 and 7, Chap. III.

prepared in 1573; this continued to be issued and used in at least sixty editions for two centuries. From this were derived translations into Danish, Italian and Latin. It is likely, therefore, that the German rendering, like the Dutch, outstripped in circulation that among the Huguenots in France, since it continued in use twice as long.[2]

When we turn to the British field we discover a decidedly different story. It is true that in 1592 an English translation of the French Psalter was issued, in the original meters and with all the tunes. But this seems to have had no wide use or influence, and today is almost unknown. A genuine train of connection, however, began over forty years earlier and can be traced into the 17th century. Yet this connection was only partial and irregular—quite unlike what has been noted in Holland and Germany. It is nevertheless worthy of somewhat detailed description.[3]

Three complete metrical Psalters in English are to be emphasized, all with a larger or smaller number of tunes, of which in each case some were borrowed from the French. These Psalters were as follows:

1. The English Psalter of 1562, usually known as that of Sternhold and Hopkins (the two poets who supplied two-thirds of the texts) and also, after 1700, as the "Old Version" (to distinguish it from the "New Version" of Tate and Brady in 1696). In spite of this and other competitions, the Old Version continued to be reprinted even until 1828.

2. The Scottish Psalter of 1564, which was largely identical with the English, but also notably divergent in both texts and tunes. This book remained in use less than a century, being displaced in 1650 by a totally different version.

3. The Psalter of Henry Ainsworth in 1612, issued at Amsterdam for the English refugees from persecution for their "separatist" opinions. This also, through no less than six editions before 1700, was widely used

---

[2] For hints as to the extensive literature upon German psalmody and hymnody, see notes 3 and 5, Chap. I.

The monumental catalogue of melodies by Zahn, which is constantly cited in Part II, being confined to Lutheran publications, omits formal reference to Lobwasser's translation from the French, but indicates that at least 19 of the French tunes passed into Lutheran use before 1600, 28 more before 1700, 19 more before 1800, and 13 more since 1800 or without date. Out of the 125 French tunes he includes at least 79.

[3] Regarding the early stages of British psalmody, see note 10, Chap. III.

in England by the Puritan party, besides being carried to America in 1620 and used at Plymouth, Massachusetts, until 1692.[4]

In studying these Psalters it is needful to recall certain points in their genesis.

The first steps were taken by Thomas Sternhold, who was a court servitor under Henry VIII and his son Edward VI (king from 1547). At a time not precisely known Sternhold undertook making metrical versions of the Psalms, supposedly, it is said, to provide something more edifying than the rough ditties in vogue among the court attendants. These versions attracted the notice of the boy king (Edward) and of others for their simple felicity. Sternhold, however, died in 1549. But he had then completed forty Psalms, most of which were printed. There is an evident analogy between his work and that of Marot, except that Sternhold was not an experienced poet and stood in a much humbler station than Marot. The latter's versions began ten to fifteen years earlier and are likely to have been known in some way in London. From internal evidence it is possible to argue that Sternhold was acquainted with them. But of this there is no external evidence.

The next stage in the story is at Geneva. Thither and to Frankfort British Protestants began to flee for safety even before Mary succeeded Edward in 1553. At Geneva Sternhold's verses were again reprinted, now with some additions by John Hopkins and William Whittingham, both Englishmen. Later John Knox, already eminent as a Scottish Protestant, was connected with further publications. William Kethe, also a Scotsman, became an active and valuable coadjutor. Thus through at least three editions was built up what is now known as the "Anglo-Genevan Psalter." Tunes were first added in 1556. By 1561 the collection contained eighty-seven Psalms, set to sixty tunes. It was evidently much influenced by the

---

[4] References to Ainsworth's remarkable book, especially on those features of it here under consideration, are notably few and meagre—occasionally exasperating. See the present writer's *Music of the Pilgrims,* Boston, 1921, which contains all the tunes, with a historical introduction and various notes (a few of which need some slight correction). The recent book of Percy Scholes, *The Puritans and Music,* London, 1934, has many remarks that bear upon this subject.

French Psalter of 1551–54, with which it corresponds in general scope, though neither texts nor tunes exactly match. Kethe and Whittingham were particularly inclined to adopt French models.

Elizabeth's accession in 1558 permitted the exiles to return home. The final stage, therefore, was at London and Edinburgh. The cleavage between parties had now become so marked that complete Psalters were wrought out by two separate groups of editors, the English led by Hopkins, the Scottish by Knox. Though the two resulting books were largely identical or similar, the English tended to avoid the French style of both verse and music, while the Scottish adhered to it to a much greater extent. They may be called twin sisters with contrasted temperaments.

The Ainsworth Psalter stands apart from the foregoing. Its date is fifty years later and in method and style it is unique. For our purpose it is enough to note that its tunes are explicitly drawn from two sources—the English Psalter, with which those for whom it was made were familiar, and the Dutch Psalter, which they had come to know in their exile. The latter source was identical with the French, as we have seen. The use of this Dutch-French material is notably intelligent and skillful.

Taking these three books together, it appears that at least 42 of the 125 French tunes in some form came into British knowledge and use, not to speak of various other lines of connection. Since all three books were in use in England during the first half of the 17th century, it is interesting to reflect that some impress was felt simultaneously by three diverse groups—the Anglican, the Presbyterian, and the Independent. To be sure, the magnitude of this impress was not relatively great. But for the time it is to be remembered.

The list of the French tunes that were thus borrowed into British use is as follows:

French	English	Scottish	Ainsworth
2	122	122	
6		85	
8			25
10		83	

Diffusion of the French Tunes

French	English	Scottish	Ainsworth
12			3=86
16		138	
19	111	111	
20		58	
21	125	125	
23			18=69
24			60
28			35=77
32			119
33		81	
35		88	
36=68	113	113	84=136
42		27	
43		142	
47		47	
50	50	50	50
66=118		118	
74		70	97
78=90	126	126	58
91		91	75
92			37
100=131=142			33=81=104
101 (part)	134	134	
102		102	
103		62	
104	104	104	55
107		107=120	
110		110	
117=127		117	
120			78
121	121	121	
124	124	124	8
128		128	
129		129	
130	130	130	7=74
132		36	
134	100	100	100
140=Dec.	Dec.		5
42 tunes	13 tunes	31 tunes	19 tunes

Out of the French tunes which Douen counts as "best," just one-half are taken—4 in all three books, 4 in both English and Scottish, 7 in the Scottish only, 6 in Ainsworth only.

The tunes borrowed are mostly in the D-mode (17 cases) or the C-mode (14 cases). The English avoids both the E- and A-modes, and Ainsworth has none in the A-mode.

In the tunes borrowed in the English Psalter there is but one that is taken without change (No. 50). The English alterations are mainly of two sorts—to adjust the meters to the eights and sixes of Common Meter, and to reduce many of the line-patterns to a series of short notes enclosed between two longs. Both these uniformities (or monotonies) were already dominant in English usage.

For example, "Old 100th" (French 134th) is now usually heard in the English redaction instead of the more stately original form. "Old 124th" ("Toulon") was first taken in its pristine five lines, but with the syncopation in the third line carefully ironed out. "Old 113th" (French 68th—the famous "Battle Song") has its meter deftly changed to Long Particular Meter.

In the Scottish Psalter, on the other hand, there are no less than thirteen tunes borrowed without change, and the general fidelity to the French is notable, except for slight adaptations in the meters. Syncopations, feminine endings and triplet feet are usually retained.

In the tunes borrowed by Ainsworth there is a mixture of precise reproduction with some effort to avoid feminine endings. In the latter cases the abbreviation is skillfully done, so that many tunes are adaptable to modern hymns.

Ps. 45 in Ainsworth is set to a melody that bears several marks of the French style, though not found in the French Psalter.

After deducting the tunes in the British books that were borrowed from the French, there remain a large number—about 100—that are not accounted for. The bulk of these came into British use through the so-called Anglo-Genevan books, so that it is evident that the genesis of these latter has historic importance in determining the rise of what we may call the British style of tune.

But regarding the personnel and method of preparing the music in the Genevan books there seems to be great uncertainty. It is likely that Whittingham was somewhat influential, since we know that later, when Dean of Durham, he took special interest in the musical service. He was probably the best scholar in the Genevan group, but how far he was practically expert in music is not clear.

It would be helpful if we knew something of who did the musical work in finishing both the British books for publication. From the analogy of the working out of the French Psalter, we infer that the focus of attention was upon the drafting of the verbal text, the service of musicians upon the melodies being held to be subordinate, if not menial.

In working over the statistical details it is to be noted that the English Psalter, as completed, differed from the Scottish in having some 15 tunes for canticles and hymns, which at first the latter eschewed. For the Psalms proper the English had about 50 tunes against about 100 in the Scottish. In this difference it may be that we have a small additional item in the general impression that during the Genevan stage a leading influence came from those who later were ranked as Puritans. It is significant that at that stage the whereabouts of Hopkins were unknown, whereas Knox was conspicuous. Even Whittingham, though conformist enough to be honored at Durham, in 1579 died excommunicate for some of his opinions. Against him were counted the facts that his rank as clergyman came from Calvin and that he had married Calvin's sister.

Many of the technical differences between the English style and the French are evident, especially from an analysis of the about 35 tunes in the English that are applied to the Psalms proper without being derived from the French. A few brief summaries are subjoined:

Meter. None of the original English meters is the same as any in the French, except that Long Meter Double (as in No. 51) is a double of the French 8888. The predominance of Common Meter (88%) laid a paralyzing hand on English hymnodic verse for at least three centuries.

Mode. The tunes almost limit themselves to two modes—one major (in about double the ratio in the French), the other more minor than modal (again much more than in the French).

Ambitus. The range of an octave or a ninth is almost universal. About half the tunes are plagal.

Identical lines. Repeats within tunes are notably few. But doublets between tunes are abundant, especially in opening and closing lines, suggesting a paucity of invention.

Diatonics and skips. The proportion of diatonic steps is slightly less than in the French. But the number of skips of a third is decidedly less. The relative frequency of skips of a fourth or fifth offsets the monotony elsewhere. The formulæ of opening and closing lines differ in nature and balance from those in the French, as well as the line-contours.

Metric patterns. In nearly 30 tunes the 8-note and 6-note lines vibrate steadily between but two patterns in each case—preferring a chain of short notes between two long ones. Two tunes (No. 77 and the Lamentation) have a steady triplet form, while triplet lines and imitations of French patterns occur in Nos. 51, 136, 137, and 148.

PART II

The Music of the Psalter

XI

The Melodies in Modern Notation

THE FOLLOWING reproduction of the traditional French tunes in modern notation is based primarily upon one of the first editions of the completed Psalter, the title page of which reads as follows:

PSEAVMES DE
DAVID

mis en rime francaise

par

Clement Marot & Theodore de Beze

Engraved device with two figures,
one seated and holding a synagogal scroll,
the other reclining below.
At the top the legend VIRTVTI FORTVNA CEDIT

A PARIS

Par Adrian le Roy & Robert Ballard
Imprimeurs du Roy

M. D. LXII

Auec privilege du Roy pour dix ans

The musical texts of this basic edition have been collated carefully with those given by Douen; with various later editions of the French Psalter; with more than one of the accepted Dutch versions; with Henri Expert's elegant *Le Psautier huguenot du XVI⁰ siècle,* 1902; and also with the tunes borrowed for British use in the early English and Scottish Psalters; and with the many that have been adopted into Lutheran use in Germany (as summarized in Zahn's great work, *Die Melodien der deutschen evangelischen Kirchen- lieder* (1888–93). The number of significant variations in all these is relatively very small. The more important are noted under the several tunes involved.

[79]

In using the music as here presented certain details of method and form need to be borne in mind. For each of these details there were sound practical reasons.

Over twenty of the tunes are set to more than one Psalm. All of these are printed here but once, each under the number of the Psalm where it first occurs. The French Psalms are numbered as in the standard Hebrew text, not as in the Greek and Latin versions.

The original notes are semibreves and minims, with a "long" at the close of the tune. These are here represented (as in Zahn) by minims and crotchets, but usually with a semibreve at the end of each phrase.

Originally there were no bars, but phrases were separated by check-marks. For the latter a half-bar is here used. Where half-stanzas occur in the verse a full bar is used to show where the tune is divisible.

Originally there were no accidentals, though in later editions they became usual. They are here set above the staff only to indicate where modification is needed to avoid the tritone or to form final cadences.[1]

Various technical facts about the structure of the tunes or their history are indicated in each case in the headings prefixed or the notes appended. Most of these points have been otherwise treated in the preceding chapters, but those pertaining to tunes borrowed are more summarily discussed in Chapter X.

[1] These added marks are mainly based upon suggestions from Dr. Percy Goetschius. They are supported by many French and Dutch editions after 1562.

I

10   10   11   11   10   10

Iambic

1539 (1542), to text by Marot

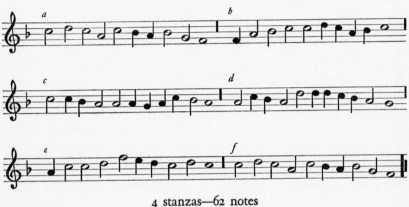

4 stanzas—62 notes

A Strassburg tune (1539, in C), somewhat altered at Geneva (1542, in F). See Douen, I, 625.

Meter not elsewhere, but used in English by Sidney for the same Psalm in imitation. On Marot's note on the verse, see Gérold, *Marot,* p. xxx.

Repeat: $a = f$ (as altered).

Ratio of short notes least of all the tunes (35%). The effective opening of lines with 5 long notes occurs in 9 tunes, all set to words by Marot.

Douen calls this tune one of the best.

From 1597 taken into Lutheran use. See Zahn, No. 3096b.

[81]

10   11   10   11   11   10   11   10

Iambic

1539 (1542), to text by Marot

6½ stanzas—85 notes

A Strassburg tune (1539, with a strange typographical discrepancy between the first half and the second), the first six lines much altered at Geneva (1542, with the early error corrected). See Douen, I, 625–26.

Douen regards the mode as minor.

Meter not elsewhere. On the quality of the verbal text, see Gérold, *Marot,* p. xxx.

Repeats: *a* = *c*, *e* = *g* (as altered).

Pattern of *a* = *c* only here and in 27. Monotone opening in *e* = *g*. Octave-leap between *d* and *e*.

Final skip in *eg* only here and in 91*e* and 112*d*.

Douen calls this tune one of the best.

Not noted in Zahn.

3

6   6   7   6   6   7   6   6   7   6   6   7

Iambic

1551, to text by Marot

4 stanzas—76 notes

The third tune used for this Psalm, replacing one from Strassburg (1539, in A, only 6 lines), followed by a second at Geneva (1542, in F, 12 lines). See Douen, I, 626, 633.

Meter as in Nunc dimittis (6 lines), and used in English by Sidney for the same Psalm in imitation.

Doublet: *k* = 97*a*.

Ratio of short notes rather high (61%). Pattern of *a* only here and in 26. Monotone opening in *i*. Several rhymes or imitations in line-ends.

Taken into English and Scottish Psalters for Ps. 122 (meter changed to 668 668 D).

From 1675 taken into Lutheran use. See Zahn, No. 8234.

[83]

4

Iambic

1542, to text by Marot

4 stanzas—86 notes

The second tune used for this Psalm, replacing one from Strassburg in the Pseudo-Roman book (in E, 5 lines only), there set for both Pss. 4 and 13. See Douen, I, 617.

Meter not elsewhere.

Douen regards the mode as minor. Compass only a sixth.

Repeat: *c* = *f* (note unusual "dip," found only here and in 11*g*, 22*c* and 65*ac*).

Monotone openings in *a, c, f, h, j*—more than in any other tune. Sundry rhymes and imitations.

From 1739 taken into Lutheran use. See Zahn, No. 7823.

$$5 = 64$$

9   8   8   9   5

Iambic

1542 (5), to text by Marot
later (64), by Beza

12, 10 stanzas—39 notes

Meter not elsewhere. First line perhaps from a secular chanson. See Douen, I, 725 (under No. 64).

Doublet: $e = 33j$.

Ratio of diatonic steps very high (91%). Monotone openings in *b* and *c*. Structure commonplace.

From 1629 taken into Lutheran use. See Zahn, No. 1796.

6

7(9)   7   6   7   7   6

Iambic

1542, to text by Marot

10 stanzas—42 notes

The text was the first of Marot's metrical translations. See Douen, I, 152, and also p. 13, note, above.

The second tune used for this Psalm, replacing one from Strassburg in the Pseudo-Roman book (in D). First line from a secular chanson. See Douen, I, 618, 724.

Meter not elsewhere—lengthened by the slur in *a*.

Douen regards the mode as minor.

Pattern of *a* unique, with syncopated ending; note the final skip in *c*. Monotone opening in *a*.

Taken into Scottish Psalter for Ps. 8 (meter changed to 886 886).

From 1576 taken into Lutheran use. See Zahn, No. 2266.

7

Iambic

1551, to text by Marot

8½ stanzas—68 notes

The third tune used for this Psalm, replacing one from 1542 (in C), the other from 1549 (in A, transposed). See Douen, I, 637–38.

Meter as in 46 = 82 and 59.

Douen regards the mode as minor.

Ratio of short notes highest of all the tunes (78%).

Not noted in Zahn.

8

II   II   IO   IO

Iambic

1542, to text by Marot

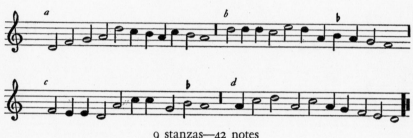

9 stanzas—42 notes

The second tune used for this Psalm, replacing one from Strassburg in the Pseudo-Roman book (in D, transposed). First line from a secular chanson. See Douen, I, 618, 724.

Meter not elsewhere in single form, but used in English by Sidney for Ps. 22 and, in double form (in the French), for 18 = 144, 32 and 45.

Douen regards the mode as minor.

Ratio of short notes low (40%), as also that of diatonic steps (66%). Different patterns for all lines (on those in *a* and *d,* see note under Ps. 1). Monotone opening in *b.*

Douen calls this tune one of the best.

Taken into Ainsworth Psalter for Ps. 25 (meter changed to 10s).

From 1592 taken into Lutheran use (usually as modal). See Zahn, No. 923.

9

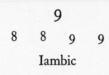

8   8   9   9

Iambic

1542, to text by Marot

20 stanzas—34 notes

The second tune used for this Psalm, replacing one from Strassburg in the Pseudo-Roman book (in 8 lines). First line from a secular chanson. See Douen, I, 618–19, 724.

Meter not elsewhere, except for first half of 35 and 73, but used in English by Sidney for Pss. 8 and 118.

Douen regards the mode as minor.

Ratio of diatonic steps low (70%). Monotone opening in *a*. Different patterns for all lines.

From 1663 taken into Lutheran use. See Zahn, No. 702.

On use by Huguenot martyrs, see Gérold, *Marot,* p. xxxi.

10

10   10   10   10   10   11   11(12)

Iambic

1551, to text by Marot

9 stanzas—73 notes

The third tune used for this Psalm, replacing one from 1542 and another (partly similar) from 1549. See Douen, I, 638.

Meter not elsewhere, but used in English by Sidney for Ps. 51. This and Ps. 11 the only ones with seven lines.

Douen regards the mode as minor.

Repeats: *ab* = *cd*. Musical rhyme between *bd* and *g*.

Ratio of diatonic steps very high (91%). Patterns mostly rare. Octave-leap from *d* to *e*.

Taken into Scottish Psalter for Ps. 83.

Not noted in Zahn.

11   10   11   10   11   10   11

Iambic

1551, to text by Marot

3½ stanzas—74 notes

The second tune used for this Psalm, replacing one from 1542 (as slightly altered in 1549). See Douen, I, 639.

Meter not elsewhere.

Douen regards the mode as minor.

Ratio of short notes high (62%). Pattern of *b* rare. Cadence in *d* unique in this mode. Note "dip" in *g* (cf. under Ps. 4).

Not noted in Zahn.

12

Iambic

1551, to text by Marot

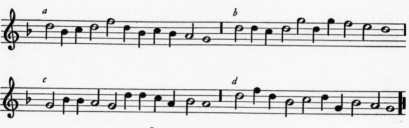

8 stanzas—42 notes

The second tune used for this Psalm, replacing one from 1542 (as slightly modified in 1549). See Douen, I, 639.

Meter as in 110 and (6 lines) in 37.

Douen regards the mode as minor.

Ratio of diatonic steps (as in 80) the lowest of all the tunes (61%). Compare opening figure with those in 27 and 74.

Douen calls this tune one of the best.

Taken into Ainsworth Psalter for Pss. 3 and 86 (meter changed to 10s). From 1779 taken into Lutheran use. See Zahn, No. 900.

13

Iambic

1542, to text by Marot

5 stanzas—43 notes

The second tune used for this Psalm, replacing one from Strassburg in the Pseudo-Roman book (two lines altered in 1549). First line from a secular chanson. See Douen, I, 618, 640, 724.

Meter not elsewhere.

Patterns of *b* (with syncopated ending), and of *a* both rare, the latter with monotone opening. Different patterns for all lines.

From 1675 taken into Lutheran use. See Zahn, No. 1791.

$14 = 53$

10   11   11   10   4

Iambic

1542 (14), to text by Marot
later (53), by Beza

7, 6 stanzas—46 notes

Slightly altered in 1549. See Douen, I, 640.

Note that this tune is set for two Psalms that are almost exact doublets in the Hebrew—a touch of scholarly precision imitated in the Scottish Psalter.

Meter not elsewhere.

Douen regards the mode as minor.

Monotone opening in *a*. Pattern of *e* only here and in 138.

Not noted in Zahn.

15

8   9   8   8   9

Iambic

1539, to text by Marot

5 stanzas—42 notes

A Strassburg tune, but somewhat recast at Geneva (1542) and one note changed later. See Douen, I, 627, 634.

Meter not elsewhere.

Compass only a sixth. Monotone openings in *a* and *c*.

Expert reads the opening of *c* and the close of *d* somewhat differently.

From 1829 taken into Lutheran use. See Zahn, No. 1793.

16

IO   II   IO   II   II   II

Iambic

1551, to text by Beza

6 stanzas—64 notes

Meter not elsewhere.

Douen regards the mode as minor.

Ratio of diatonic steps low (71%). Patterns of *a, c,* and *f* rare. Monotone opening in *c*. Syncopated endings in *c* and *f*, with imitation.

Taken unchanged into Scottish Psalter for Ps. 138.
Not noted in Zahn.

$$17 = 63 = 70$$

8   9   9   8   9   8   8   9

Iambic

1551, to texts by Beza

7, 6, 2 stanzas—68 notes

Full meter not elsewhere, but second half as in 141, and first half used in English by Sidney for Ps. 37.

Several imitations in openings and ends of lines.

From 1639, taken into Lutheran use. See Zahn, No. 5927.

18 = 144

| II | II | IO | IO | II | II | IO | IO |

Iambic

1544 (18), to text by Marot
later (144), by Beza

13⅔, 6½ stanzas—84 notes

The text of 18 is unique in having a partial stanza at the beginning (4 lines) as well as at the end (6 lines), necessitating a tune divisible at two points. Note that the tune is set for two Psalms that in Hebrew are in part close doublets (see under 14).

Meter as in 32 and 45 (also half as in 8).

Douen regards the mode as minor.

Ratio of diatonic steps high (88%). Several imitations.

From 1848 taken (in the form as here) into Lutheran use. See Zahn, No. 8336.

6   6   6   6   6   6   6   6   7   6   6   7

Iambic

1542, to text by Marot

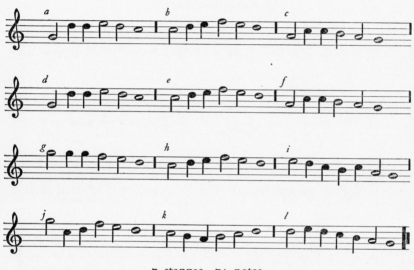

7 stanzas—74 notes

Replaced a Strassburg tune (1539). Somewhat altered in 1549. See Douen, I, 620, 640–41.

Full meter not elsewhere, but second half as in Nunc dimittis.

Repeats: *abc = def* and *be = h*.

Ratio of short notes very low (38%); that of diatonic steps high (89%). Octave-leaps between *f* and *g* and between *i* and *j*. Only two patterns.

Taken into English Psalter for Ps. 111 (all patterns changed) and into Scottish, also for Ps. 111 (patterns unchanged).

From 1606 taken into Lutheran use. See Zahn, No. 8232.

20

9　6　9　6　9　7　9　7

Iambic

1551, to text by Beza

4½ stanzas—62 notes

First and second lines may be taken from a secular chanson supposed to be by Marot. See Douen, I, 724–25.

Full meter not elsewhere, but second half used in English by Sidney for Ps. 42.

Douen regards the mode as minor.

Doublets: b = 40hi and h = 107h.

Ratio of short notes very high (74%), and that of diatonic steps very high (94%). Syncopated ending in a and sundry imitations. Patterns of a, b, d rare.

Taken into Scottish Psalter for Ps. 58 (meter changed to C.M.D.). From 1629 taken into Lutheran use. See Zahn, No. 5940.

21

8   7   7   8   6   6

Iambic

1551, to text by Beza

13 stanzas—42 notes

Meter not elsewhere.

Doublet: $a = 84g$.

Simple melody, but with dextrous contrasts between first and second halves. Readily adaptable to modern harmony.

Taken into English and Scottish Psalters for Ps. 125 (meter changed to 8888 66, the English with line-end of c changed).

Not noted in Zahn.

10   10   10   5   II   II   II   4

Iambic

1542, to text by Marot

15½ stanzas—72 notes

The second tune used for this Psalm, replacing one from Strassburg in the Pseudo-Roman book. Lines *f* and *g* recast in 1549. See Douen, I, 620–21, 641.

Meter not elsewhere, but last half used in English by Sidney for Ps. 125. Douen regards the mode as minor.

Pattern of *h* only here and in 101 and 138. Monotone openings in *e* and *f* (1549). Note "dips" in *a, c* (cf. under 4), *e, f*.

Not noted in Zahn.

II · II · II · II · II · II

Iambic

1544, to text by Marot

3 stanzas—66 notes

Meter not elsewhere. All lines with feminine endings.

Monotone openings in *a* and *c*. Octave-leap between *e* and *f*. Only two patterns.

Douen calls this tune one of the best.

Taken into Ainsworth Psalter for Pss. 18 = 69 (meter changed to 10s throughout).

From 1613 taken into Lutheran use. See Zahn, No. 3199.

$$24 = 62 = 95 = 111$$

8   8   9   8   8   9

Iambic

1542 (24), to text by Marot
62, 95, 111 later by Beza

5, 8, 7, 6 stanzas—50 notes

The second tune used for this Psalm, replacing a Strassburg tune in the Pseudo-Roman book, and somewhat recast in 1549. See Douen, I, 621, 641–42.

Meter as in 113.

Douen regards the mode as minor.

Patterns of *a* unique and of *f* rare. Monotone opening in *d*.

Douen calls this tune one of the best.

Taken into Ainsworth Psalter for Ps. 60 (meter changed to L.P.M.). From 1730 taken into Lutheran use. See Zahn, No. 2665.

8   7   8   7   7   8   7   8

Trochaic

1551, to text by Marot

10 stanzas—60 notes

The third tune used for this Psalm, replacing one from Strassburg (1539, in D), recast at Geneva (1542), and the other from 1549 (in D, transposed). The melody resembles an old Flemish song. See Douen, I, 627, 636, 648, 720–21 and Gérold, *Marot,* p. xxxi.

Meter nearly as in 42, and used in English by Sidney for Ps. 44.

Repeats: *ab = cd.*

Patterns of *a = c* and of *f* rare.

Douen calls this tune one of the best.

From 1642 taken into Lutheran use. See Zahn, No. 6678.

26

6 6 8 7 7 8

Iambic

1551, to text by Beza

12 stanzas—42 notes

Meter not elsewhere, but compare 668 668 in Sidney for Ps. 74.
Pattern of *a* only here and in 3.

Curiously, *a* and *f* somewhat resemble lines in Hasler's air (1601),
usually set to "O Haupt voll Blut und Wunden."

From 1770 taken into Lutheran use. See Zahn, No. 2185.

11   10   11   10   10   10   10   10

Iambic

1551, to text by Beza

7 stanzas—82 notes

Full meter not elsewhere, but first half as in 12 and 110, and second half as in 93

Douen regards the mode as minor.

Repeats: *ab* = *cd*. Rhyme between *bd* and *h*.

Pattern of *e* and *g* only here and in 2. Octave-leap between *d* and *e*. The opening resembles those of 74 and 12 (minor).

Douen calls this tune one of the best.

From 1730 taken into Lutheran use. See Zahn, No. 6192.

28 = 109

9   9   9   9   8   8

Iambic

1551, to texts by Beza

6, 18 stanzas—52 notes

Meter not elsewhere.

Pattern of *a* and *d* unique, with syncopated ending.

Taken into Ainsworth Psalter for Pss. 35 = 77.
Not noted in Zahn.

29

7   7   7   7   8   8   8   8

Trochaic

1551, to text by Beza

5 stanzas—60 notes

Full meter not elsewhere, but first half as in 136. Compare meter used in English by Sidney for Ps. 69.

Repeat: $e = f$.

Patterns related to those of 25 and 42.

Not noted in Zahn.

$$30 = 76 = 139$$

8   8   8   8   9   9

Iambic

1551, to texts by Beza

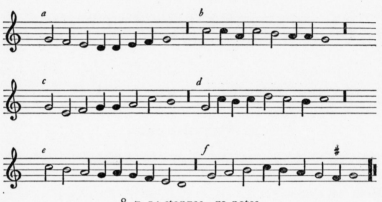

8, 7, 14 stanzas—50 notes

Meter not elsewhere.

Doublet: $e = 58d$.

Different patterns throughout, that of f only here and in 22. Syncopated endings in d and f.

From 1587 taken into Lutheran use. See Zahn, No. 2652, where in c the last note is read one step lower.

$$31 = 71$$

9   6   6   9   7   7

Iambic

1551, to texts by Beza

19, 18 stanzas—44 notes

This tune is set for two Psalms that in Hebrew are doublets in small part (see under 14 and 18).

Meter not elsewhere.

Ratio of diatonic steps high (89%). Pattern of *a* rare, with syncopated ending.

Not noted in Zahn.

11   11   10   10   11   11   10   10

Iambic

1549, to text by Marot

5½ stanzas—84 notes

The third tune used for this Psalm, replacing one from Strassburg (1539, 4 lines), the other from Geneva (1542, 8 lines). First line from a secular chanson. See Douen, I, 621–22, 642, 725.

Meter as in 18 and 45.

Ratio of diatonic steps high (88%). Pattern of *a* rare (see under 1). Monotone openings in *e, f, g*. Also octave-leap between *d* and *e*.

Douen justly calls this tune one of the best.

Taken into Ainsworth Psalter for Ps. 119. Its omission from both English and Scottish is surprising.

From 1771 taken into Lutheran use. See Zahn, No. 6225.

$$33 = 67$$

9 8 9 8 6 6 5 6 6 5

Iambic   Trochaic

1543, to text by Marot,
later (67), by Beza

11, 3 stanzas—68 notes

Full meter not elsewhere, but quatrain as in 140 = Decalogue.

Repeats: *ab = cd* and *e = f*. Doublet: *j = 5e*.

The only other case of a tune divided into two sections in contrasted rhythm is that for Ps. 48.

Douen calls this tune one of the best.

Taken into Scottish Psalter for Ps. 81 (first two lines somewhat changed).

From 1618 taken into Lutheran use. See Zahn, No. 7990.

34

10½ stanzas—56 notes

First line from a secular chanson. See Douen, I, 725.

Meter not elsewhere, but used in English by Sidney for the same Psalm in imitation.

Patterns with syncopated endings in *c* and *h,* the latter unique. Monotone opening in *b* (perhaps imitated in *g*).

Quoted by Zahn (No. 5230), but without data of use.

35

8   8   9   9   8   8   8   8

Iambic

1551, to text by Beza

13 stanzas—66 notes

Meter as in 73, but first half as in 9 and second half as in 100 and 134. The latter, known in English as L.M., is not used by Sidney.

Syncopated ending in *a*. Octave-leap between *f* and *g*. Contrasted contours in *e* and *f*.

Taken into Scottish Psalter for Ps. 88 (meter changed to L.M.D.). From 1639 taken into Lutheran use. See Zahn, No. 5881.

$$36 = 68$$

8 8 7 8 8 7 8 8 7 8 8 7

Iambic

1539, to text by Marot
later (68), by Beza

5, 16½ stanzas—92 notes

A Strassburg tune (1539), but with two notes altered in 1542 and 1549. It first appeared in 1525 (for Ps. 119) under Greiter's name, and became well known. In French for over twenty years it was associated only with Ps. 36 (by Marot), but soon after 1560 its use was extended to Ps. 68, with certain militant stanzas through which it became a favorite Huguenot war-song during the civil conflicts preceding 1572, so that in recent times it has been dubbed "the Huguenot Marseillaise." See Douen, I, 658.

Meter not elsewhere, but half-meter used in English by Sidney for Ps. 32. The longest of the tunes (92 notes).

Repeats: *abc* = *def* and *g* = *h* (as altered).

Doublets: *ad* = 138*j* and *l* = 122*d* and Nunc dimittis *f*.

Ratio of short notes very high (70%). Only two patterns. Monotone opening in *g* = *h*. Imitation between *j* and *k*. Octave-leap between *f* and *g*.

Douen emphasizes this tune as one of the best.

Taken into English and Scottish Psalters for Ps. 113 (meter changed to L.P.M.D.); also into Ainsworth for Pss. 84 = 136. It remained in English use till after 1800. In New England it was still known in 1799 (see *Hartford Selection,* Hymns 12 and 15).

From 1525 taken into Lutheran use. See Zahn, No. 8303, and also Gérold, *Les plus anciennes mélodies,* pp. 61–62, with notes as to extensive polyphonic use, as by J. S. Bach in his Matthew Passion (end of first Part) and in one of his Choralvorspiele. Zahn reads the last note of *g* two degrees lower (as in 1539) and also has a different reading for *i.* Cf. Douen, I, 628.

37

11   10   11   10   11   10

Iambic

1549, to text by Marot

20 stanzas—63 notes

The second tune for this Psalm, replacing one from 1542 (in C). See Douen, I, 643.

Meter not elsewhere.

Douen regards the mode as minor.

Repeat: *b = d.*

Ratio of diatonic steps high (89%). Only two patterns. Monotone opening in *a, b = d.* Octave-leap between *c* and *d.*

From 1566 taken into Lutheran use. See Zahn, No. 3159, where he reads the first note of *c* one degree higher, which is probably right.

[117]

38

8   4   7   8   4   7

Trochaic

1542, to text by Marot

22 stanzas—38 notes

Slightly altered in 1549. See Douen, I, 643.
Meter as in 61.
Douen regards the mode as minor.

From 1629 taken into Lutheran use. See Zahn, No. 2531.

39

10   8   10   8   10   8

Iambic

1551, to text by Beza

8 stanzas—54 notes

Meter not elsewhere, but used in English by Sidney for the same Psalm in imitation.

Douen regards the mode as minor.

Syncopated endings in *b* and *d*.

Not noted in Zahn.

10   8   8   10   7   7   6   6   6   6

Iambic

1551, to text by Beza

8 stanzas—74 notes

Meter not elsewhere.

Repeats: $e = f$ and $h = i$. Doublet: $hi = 20h$.

Pattern of *a* rare, with syncopated ending. Octave-leap between *f* and *g*.

Not noted in Zahn.

10   6   10   6   10   6   10   6

Iambic

1551, to text by Beza

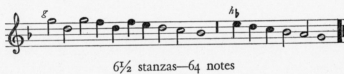

6½ stanzas—64 notes

Meter not elsewhere, but used in English by Sidney for the same Psalm in imitation.

Douen regards the mode as minor.

Doublet: $h = 149h$.

Pattern of c only here and in 145, with syncopated ending. Initial "dip" in g unique (but cf. 61d).

Not noted in Zahn.

42

8   7   8   7   7   7   8   8

Trochaic

1551, to text by Beza

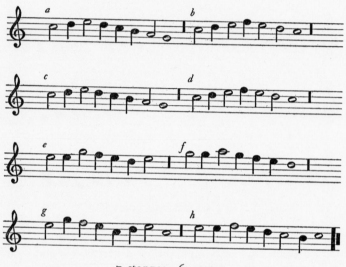

7 stanzas—60 notes

Meter much as in 25, and used in English by Sidney for the same Psalm in imitation (also for Ps. 44). First line perhaps from a secular chanson. See Douen, I, 725.

Repeats: *ab = cd*.

Patterns related to those of 25 and 29. Ratio of diatonic steps very high (92%). Syncopated ending in *h*.

Douen calls this tune one of the best.

Taken into Scottish Psalter for Ps. 27 (meter changed to L.M.D., with rhythm reversed).

Not noted in Zahn.

9   8   9   9   8   6

Iambic

1544, to text by Marot

5 stanzas—49 notes

Meter not elsewhere.

Ratio of diatonic steps very high (91%). Patterns of *b* and *c* rare, with syncopated endings. Monotone openings in *c* and *d*. Different patterns for all lines.

Taken into Scottish Psalter for Ps. 142, almost unchanged.
Not noted in Zahn.

44

Iambic

1551, to text by Beza

13 stanzas—68 notes

Meter not elsewhere.

Syncopated ending in *d* and several imitations or contrasts.

Quoted by Zahn (No. 6117a), but without data of use.

45

Iambic

1544, to text by Marot

8 stanzas—84 notes

Meter as in 18 and 32 and half-meter as in 8.
Note the sweeping contours in most of the lines.

Not noted in Zahn.

$$46 = 82$$

9   9   8   8   9   9   8   8

Iambic

1551, to text by Marot,
later (82), by Beza

5½, 4 stanzas—68 notes

Meter as in 7 and 59.

Repeat: $e = f$. Doublet: $c = 126g$.

Ratio of short notes above average (59%). Only two patterns. Much imitation in line-ends.

From 1771 taken into Lutheran use. See Zahn, No. 6118.

[126]

47

Anapæstic

1551, to text by Beza

4½ stanzas—60 notes

Meter not elsewhere, though cf. that of 81.
Repeat: $f = l$. Doublets: $c = 81ac$ and $g = 81de$.
Lines group readily in pairs, making 10s, 6 lines.
Ratio of diatonic steps high (87%). Only two patterns.
Douen calls this tune one of the best.

Taken into Scottish Psalter for the same Psalm.
From 1629 taken into Lutheran use. See Zahn, No. 8337.

8   8   9   9   7   7   8   8   8   8

Iambic   Trochaic

1562, to text by Beza

5½ stanzas—80 notes

Probably based on a secular chanson. See Douen, I, 723. The first melody in the third or final group (1562).

Meter not elsewhere, but on the quatrain see under Ps. 9. On contrasted rhythms, see under Ps. 33.

Repeats: $a = b$ $c = d$ $g = h$.

Note several monotone pairs in $a = b$ and i.

Quoted by Zahn (No. 7988), but without data of use.

49

IO IO IO IO IO IO II II

Iambic

1562, to text by Beza

7 stanzas—82 notes

Meter not elsewhere, but used in English by Sidney for Ps. 105.

Monotone opening in *c.* Octave-leap between *g* and *h,* a peculiar case at that point in the tune.

Not noted in Zahn.

50

Iambic

1544, to text by Marot

9 stanzas—62 notes

Meter not elsewhere.

Repeat: *c = d*—both with monotone openings.

Contrast in contour between *e* and *f*.

Taken without change into English, Scottish and Ainsworth Psalters,
all for the same Psalm.

Quoted by Zahn (No. 3094), but notes only use by Bohemian Brethren
from 1566.

51 = 69

10   11   11   10   10   11   10   11

Iambic

1551 (51), to text by Marot
later (69), by Beza

9½, 14 stanzas—84 notes

The third tune used for this Psalm, replacing one from Strassburg (1539, in A), the other from Geneva (1542, in D). See Douen, I, 623, 649.

Full meter not elsewhere, but first half as in 74 and second half as in 129.

Douen calls this tune one of the best.

From 1730 taken into Lutheran use. See Zahn, No. 6151.
On use by Huguenot martyrs, see Gérold, *Marot,* p. xxxii.

52

9 6 9 6 8 6

Iambic

1562, to text by Beza

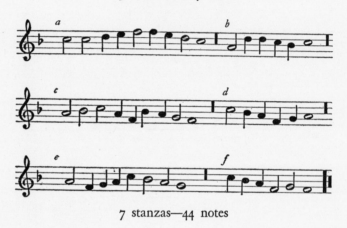

7 stanzas—44 notes

Meter not elsewhere.
Pattern of *a* unique and peculiar.
Not noted in Zahn.

53

For 53 see 14

8   9   9   8   8   9   9   8

Iambic

1562, to text by Beza

3½ stanzas—68 notes

Full meter not elsewhere, but half-meter used in English by Sidney for Ps. 37.

Not noted in Zahn.

55

9 9 9 8 8 9

Iambic

1562, to text by Beza

14 stanzas—52 notes

Meter not elsewhere.
Ratio of short notes low (44%).

Not noted in Zahn.

56

10 10 10 7 11 11 11 6

Iambic

1562, to text by Beza

6 stanzas—76 notes

First line from a secular chanson. See Douen, I, 725.

Meter not elsewhere.

Pattern of *a* unique. Monotone opening in *g*. The opening figure only here and in 66 and 89.

Not noted in Zahn.

57

Iambic

1562, to text by Beza

7 stanzas—52 notes

Meter not elsewhere.

Range of melody is high in relation to the final. On pattern of *a,* see under Ps. 1.

Not noted in Zahn.

58

9   8   8   9   8   8

Iambic

1562, to text by Beza

8 stanzas—50 notes

Meter not elsewhere.

Doublet: $d = 30e$.

Ratio of short notes very low (40%). Note contrast in contour between c and d.

From 1779 taken into Lutheran use. See Zahn, No. 2748.

Expert reads the first note two degrees lower.

59

9   9   8   8   9   9   8   8

Iambic

1562, to text by Beza

10 stanzas—68 notes

Meter as in 7 and 46 = 82.

Ratio of short notes high (62%). Only three patterns. Ratio of diatonic steps very low (65%). Note monotone pairs in *a*, *b*, *g*, and several imitative endings.

Not noted in Zahn.

$$60 = 108$$

8   8   8   8   8   8   9   9

Iambic

1562, to texts by Beza

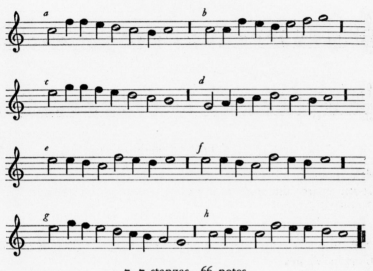

7, 7 stanzas—66 notes

Note that this tune is set for two Psalms that in the Hebrew are largely close doublets (see under 14).

Full meter not elsewhere, but half-meters reversed in 35 (q.v.).

Repeat: $e = f$.

Ratio of short notes low (42%), but of diatonic steps high (88%). Syncopated endings in *a* and *d*.

Not noted in Zahn.

61

8 4 7 8 4 7

Trochaic

1562, to text by Beza

7 stanzas—38 notes

Meter as in 38.
Douen regards the mode as minor.
Doublet: $c = 146f$.
Syncopated ending in f.

From 1629 taken into Lutheran use. See Zahn, No. 3532, but note corrections in V, 393.

62

For 62 see 24

63

For 63 see 17

64

For 64 see 5

65 = 72

9   6   9   6   9   6   9   6

Iambic

1544 (72), to text by Marot,
later (65), by Beza

10½, 9 stanzas—60 notes

Partly based on a secular chanson. See Douen, I, 722–23.
Meter not elsewhere.
Douen regards the mode as minor.
Ratio of diatonic steps high (88%). Note monotone opening and "dip"
in *a* = *c* (on the latter see under Ps. 4).
Douen calls this tune one of the best.

From 1618 taken into Lutheran use. See Zahn, No. 5933.

[141]

$66 = 98 = 118$

9   8   9   8   9   8   9   8

Iambic

1543 (118), to text by Marot,
later (66, 98), by Beza

14, 9½, 4 stanzas—68 notes

Full meter not elsewhere, but half as in 140 = Decalogue.
Repeats: $a = c$ and $d = h$.
Ratio of short notes high (62%). Opening figure only here and in 56a
and 89ab.
Douen calls this tune one of the best.

Taken into Scottish Psalter for Ps. 118 (d made to imitate b).
From 1566 taken into Lutheran use. See Zahn, No. 6002.

67

For 67 see 33

68

For 68 see 36

69

For 69 see 51

70

For 70 see 17

71

For 71 see 31

72

For 72 see 65

73

Iambic

1551, to text by Beza

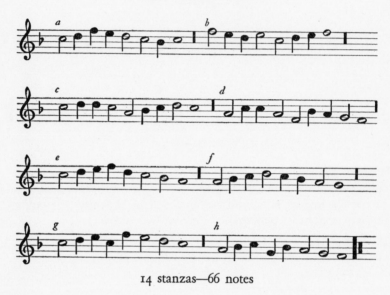

14 stanzas—66 notes

First line from a secular chanson. See Douen, I, 726.

Meter as in 35 (see notes there).

Pattern of *f* only here and in 13 and 24. Syncopated ending in *a*.

From 1826 taken into Lutheran use. See Zahn, No. 5882.

$$74 = 116$$

Iambic

1562, to texts by Beza

22, 11 stanzas—42 notes

Meter not elsewhere.

Douen regards the mode as major.

Form of opening as in 27 and recalling that of 12 (minor). Compass only a sixth. Only two patterns.

Taken into Ainsworth Psalter for Ps. 97 (meter changed to 10s). From 1656 taken into Lutheran use. See Zahn, No. 859.

75

7 7 7 7 7 7

Trochaic

1562, to text by Beza

6 stanzas—42 notes

Meter as in 135.
Doublet: *e* = 135*e*.

From 1707 taken into Lutheran use. See Zahn, No. 3333.

76

For 76 see 30

77 = 86

8   8   7   7   8   8   7   7

Trochaic

1543 (86), to text by Marot,
later (77), by Beza

8½, 11 stanzas—60 notes

First line from a secular chanson. See Douen, I, 726.
Meter not elsewhere.
Douen regards the mode as minor.
Repeats: *a = b, cd = gh, e = f.*
Ratio of diatonic steps very high (92%). Only two patterns.
Douen calls this tune one of the best.

From 1587 taken into Lutheran use. See Zahn, No. 6863.

78 = 90

II   II   II   II   IO   IO

Iambic

1531 (90), to text by Beza,
later (78), by Beza

36, 9 stanzas—64 notes

First line from a secular chanson. See Douen, I, 726.

Meter not elsewhere.

Douen regards the mode as minor.

Ratio of diatonic steps very low (62%). Several interesting skip figures.

Pattern of *b* only here and in 129, with syncopated ending.

Douen calls this tune one of the best.

Taken into English and Scottish Psalters for Ps. 126 (meter of first four
lines expanded to 12s). Also into Ainsworth for Ps. 58 (meter of the
lines condensed to 10s).

From 1587 taken into Lutheran use. See Zahn, No. 3198.

79

Iambic

1544, to text by Marot

6 stanzas—82 notes

Full meter not elsewhere, but second section as in Nunc dimittis; in English Sidney uses first section for Ps. 121 and second for Ps. 3.
Douen regards the mode as modal, perhaps unwisely.
Repeat: *e* = *f*, and last part of *a* and *d* echoed in *g* and *j*.
On pattern of *a*, see under Ps. 1.

From 1787 taken into Lutheran use. See Zahn, No. 7849.

80

9   9   8   8   8   8

Iambic

1562, to text by Beza

11 stanzas—50 notes

Meter as in 94 and 105.
Repeat: *c* = *d*. Doublet: *e* = 148*c*.
Ratio of diatonic steps very low (61%). Syncopated ending in *e*.

Not noted in Zahn.

81

5   6   5   5   5   6

Trochaic

1562, to text by Beza

18 stanzas—32 notes

Meter not elsewhere, but resembles that of 47.

Repeats: $a = c$ and $d = e$. Doublets: $ac = 47c$ and $de = 47g$.

Diatonic steps throughout, as in no other tune. On patterns cf. 33, 47, and 99.

From 1710 taken into Lutheran use. See Zahn, No. 3263.

82

For 82 see 46

83

8 8 9 9 9 9

Iambic

1562, to text by Beza

10 stanzas—52 notes

Meter not elsewhere.
Doublet: $c = 147d$.

From 1817 taken into Lutheran use. See Zahn, No. 2689.

84

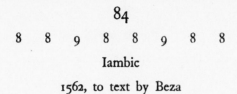

8 8 9 8 8 9 8 8

Iambic

1562, to text by Beza

6 stanzas—66 notes

Full meter not elsewhere, but that of first six lines in 24 and 113.
Repeat: $d = e$. Doublets: $de = 105cd$ and $g = 21e$.

From 1738 taken into Lutheran use. See Zahn, No. 5868 (with single
deviations in reading of b and f).

IO   IO   IO   IO   IO   IO   IO   IO

Iambic

1562, to text by Beza

4 stanzas—80 notes

Full meter not elsewhere, but used in English by Sidney for 9 Psalms. Half-meter as in 93, and in Sidney for Ps. 111.

Pattern of *c* rare, with syncopated ending.

Not noted in Zahn.

Expert reads *e* differently and first three notes of *f*.

86

For 86 see 77

87

II　　IO　　IO　　II

Iambic

1562, to text by Beza

5 stanzas—42 notes

Meter not elsewhere.
Different patterns for all lines.

Not noted in Zahn.

88

8   9   9   8   9   9

Iambic

1562, to text by Beza

11 stanzas—52 notes

Meter not elsewhere.
Douen regards the mode as minor.
Only three patterns.

From 1675 taken into Lutheran use. See Zahn, No. 2725.

89

12   12   13   13   13   13

Iambic

1562, to text by Beza

20 stanzas—76 notes

Meter not elsewhere, but cf. one in English by Sidney for Ps. 141. All the lines may be regarded as divisible into two, especially as the first half of *f* has a syncopated ending.

Repeat: *a* = *b*.

Patterns all unique.

From 1587 taken into Lutheran use. See Zahn, No. 3211.

90

For 90 see 78

8   7 (8)   8   7 (8)   8   7   8   7

Iambic

1539, to text by Marot

8 stanzas—62 notes

Originally a Strassburg tune (1539), but considerably recast in 1542 and again in 1549. See Douen, I, 628–29, 635–36.

Full meter, both of words and tune (with slurs), not elsewhere, but half-meter of words used in English by Sidney for Pss. 19 and 21.

Douen regards the mode as minor.

Repeats: ac = bd.

Ratio of short notes high (63%), but that of diatonic steps low (71%). Octave-leap between e and f. Final skip in e only here and in 2eg and 112d.

Taken into Scottish Psalter for the same Psalm and into Ainsworth for Ps. 75.

From 1588 taken into Lutheran use. See Zahn, No. 5694.

On effect of this Psalm on Beza, see Gérold, *Marot,* pp. xxxii–iii.

92

7   6   6   7   7   6   6   7

Iambic

1562, to text by Beza

8 stanzas—52 notes

Meter not elsewhere.
Douen regards the mode as minor.
Monotone openings in *a* and *c*.

Taken into Ainsworth Psalter for Ps. 37.   *No.   No. 93*
Not noted in Zahn.

93

Iambic

1562, to text by Beza

4 stanzas—40 notes

Single meter not elsewhere, but doubled in 85. The single form is used in English by Sidney for Ps. 111 and the double often.
Different patterns for all lines.

Taken, unchanged, into Ainsworth Psalter for Ps. 37.
From 1629 taken into Lutheran use. See Zahn, No. 819.

94

9   9   8   8   8   8

Iambic

1562, to text by Beza

12 stanzas—50 notes

Meter as in 80 and 105.

Not noted in Zahn.

95

For 95 see 24

96

9   9   8   8   9

Iambic

1562, to text by Beza

9 stanzas—43 notes

First line from a secular chanson.
Meter not elsewhere.
Douen regards the mode as minor.
Monotone opening in *a*.

Not noted in Zahn.

97

6   6   7   7   6   6   6   6   6

Iambic

1562, to text by Beza

7 stanzas—56 notes

First line from a secular chanson.

Meter not elsewhere. The only tune with 9 lines.

Repeats: *e* = *f* and *g* = *h*. Doublet: *a* = 3*k*.

Ratio of diatonic steps low.

From 1629 taken into Lutheran use. See Zahn, No. 7191.

[163]

98

For 98 see 66

99

5   5   5   5   5   5   6   6

Trochaic

1562, to text by Beza

8 stanzas—42 notes

Meter not elsewhere, though resembling that of 33, 47, and 81. Patterns all rare.

From 1787 taken into Lutheran use. See Zahn, No. 6237.

$$100 = 131 = 142$$

8   8   8   8

Iambic

1551 (131), to text by Beza,
later (100, 142), by Beza

4, 4, 7 stanzas—32 notes

Meter as in 134.

Ratio of diatonic steps low (71%). Pattern of *a* unique, with syncopated ending.

Douen calls this tune one of the best.

Taken into Ainsworth Psalter for Pss. 33 = 81 = 104.
From 1598 taken into Lutheran use. See Zahn, No. 367.

101

11 11 10 4

Iambic

1551, to text by Beza

8 stanzas—36 notes

The second tune used for this Psalm, replacing one from 1543. First line from a secular chanson. See Douen, I, 645, 727.

Meter not elsewhere.

Different patterns for all lines, that of *d* only here and in 22.

Douen calls this tune one of the best.

Two lines, much changed, taken into English and Scottish Psalters for Ps. 134.

From 1587 taken into Lutheran use. See Zahn, No. 919, with slight change of pattern at end of *c*.

102

8   8   7   7   8   8   8   8

Trochaic

1562, to text by Beza

16 stanzas—62 notes

Full meter not elsewhere, but second half as in 100 and 134.
Only two patterns.

Taken into Scottish Psalter for the same Psalm (meter changed to
L.M.D., with rhythm reversed).

Not noted in Zahn.

103

Iambic

1539, to text by Marot

II stanzas—64 notes

A Strassburg tune, only slightly altered in $c = f$. First line from a secular chanson. See Douen, I, 629, 728.

Meter not elsewhere.

Repeat: $c = f$.

Ratio of diatonic steps high (88%). Only two patterns (on that of $c = f$, see under Ps 1).

Douen calls this tune one of the best.

Taken into Scottish Psalter for Ps. 62 (with but trivial change in pattern).

From 1649 taken into Lutheran use. See Zahn, No. 3137.

Iambic

1539 (1542), to text by Marot

17½ stanzas—84 notes

The first half is a Strassburg tune in the Pseudo-Roman book, ably increased at Geneva (1542) to eight lines. First line from a secular chanson. See Douen, I, 629–30, 728.

Meter not elsewhere.

On patterns of *a, b, d,* see under Ps. 1. Monotone openings in *e, f, h,* Octave-leap between *d* and *e*. Many free skips.

Taken into English and Scottish Psalters for the same Psalm, and into Ainsworth for Ps. 55.

Not noted in Zahn.

105

9 9 8 8 8 8

Iambic

1562, to text by Beza

24 stanzas—50 notes

Meter as in 80 and 94.
Repeat: $c = d$. Doublets: $cd = 84de$ and $f = 133c$.
Syncopated endings in $c = d$.

From 1740 taken into Lutheran use. See Zahn, No. 2995, with first note of *cd* three degrees higher.

106

8   8   9   8   9   8

Iambic

1562, to text by Beza

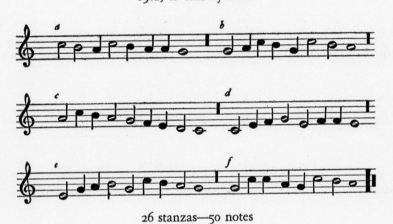

26 stanzas—50 notes

Meter not elsewhere.
Pattern of *a* only here and in 121.

Not noted in Zahn.

7 6 7 6 6 7 6 7

Iambic

1544; to text by Marot

21½ stanzas—52 notes

First line possibly from a secular chanson. See Douen, I, 727.
Meter not elsewhere.

Douen regards the mode as minor.

Repeat: $a = c$. Doublet: $b = 20h$.

Ratio of short notes very low (38%). Only three patterns. Skip-sequence in $a = c$ unique. Octave-leap between d and e.

Taken into Scottish Psalter for the same Psalm (meter changed to C.M.D.).

From 1640 taken into Lutheran use. See Zahn, No. 5261.

108

For 108 see 60

109

For 109 see 28

110

11   10   11   10

Iambic

1551, to text by Marot

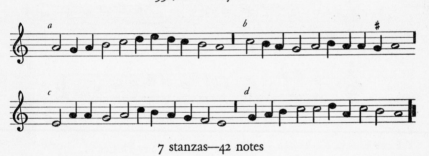

7 stanzas—42 notes

The second tune used for this Psalm, replacing one from 1542. See Douen, I, 645.

Meter as in 12.

Douen regards the mode as minor.

Ratio of diatonic steps very high (89%).

Taken into Scottish Psalter for the same Psalm (meter changed to 10s). From 1778 taken into Lutheran use. See Zahn, No. 901.

III

For III see 24

112

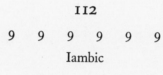

Iambic

1562, to text by Beza

6 stanzas—54 notes

Meter not elsewhere.

Douen regards the mode as minor.

All lines with feminine endings. Final skip in *d* only here and in 2*eg* and 91*e*. Octave-leap between *d* and *e*.

From 1679 taken into Lutheran use. See Zahn, No. 3060.

113

8   8   9   8   8   9

Iambic

1551, to text by Marot

5 stanzas—50 notes

The third tune used for this Psalm, replacing one from Strassburg in the Pseudo-Roman book and another from Geneva (both 1542), the latter somewhat recast in 1549. First line from a secular chanson. See Douen, I, 623–24, 643–44, 727.

Meter as in 24.

Ratio of diatonic steps low (70%).

From 1787 taken into Lutheran use. See Zahn, No. 2663.

114

Iambic

1539, to text by Marot

4 stanzas—54 notes

A Strassburg tune, somewhat altered in 1542 and 1549. See Douen, I, 630, 634.

Meter as in 115, the two Psalms being at first set to the same tune. Doublet: $f = 149d$.

Pattern of *ab* unique. Ratio of diatonic steps very high (90%). Monotone openings in *a* and *d*.

Not noted in Zahn.

115

10   10   7   10   10   7

Iambic

1542, to text by Marot

11 stanzas—54 notes

Meter as in 114 (q. v.).

Not noted in Zahn.

116

For 116 see 74

117 = 127

8   8   8   8   8   8

Iambic

1551, to texts by Beza

1, 5 stanzas—48 notes

First line from a secular chanson. See Douen, I, 727.
Meter not elsewhere, but used in English by Sidney for Ps. 86.
Ratio of diatonic steps very high (91%). Syncopated ending in f.

Taken, unchanged, into Scottish Psalter for the same Psalm.
Not noted in Zahn.
Sung in 1587 at the battle of Coutras.

118

For 118 see 66

119

10   11   10   11   10   11

Iambic

1551, to text by Beza

88 stanzas—63 notes

First line from a secular chanson. See Douen, I, 727.

Meter not elsewhere.

Ratio of short notes and diatonic steps both high (58% and 88%).
Only two patterns.

Douen calls this tune one of the best.

From 1829 taken into Lutheran use. See Zahn, No. 3114.

120

9 9 9 9 9 9 8 8

Iambic

1551, to text by Beza

3 stanzas—70 notes

Meter not elsewhere.

Ratio of short notes high (63%). Pattern of *b* rare, with syncopated ending. Monotone opening in *e*. Note contour-contrasts in first half.

Taken into Ainsworth Psalter for Ps. 78 (meter changed to 10s, with uniform patterns).

Not noted in Zahn.

121

8   6   6   8   7   7

Iambic

1551, to text by Beza

4 stanzas—42 notes

Meter not elsewhere.

Ratio of diatonic steps very high (94%). Different patterns for all lines, those of *a* and *f* rare. Syncopated ending in *d*.

Taken into English and Scottish Psalters for the same Psalm (all patterns changed in the former, none in the latter).

From 1629 taken into Lutheran use. See Zahn, No. 2350.

8　　8　　8　　8　　8　　8　　9　　8　　8　　9

Iambic

1551, to text by Beza

2 stanzas—82 notes

Full meter not elsewhere, but first section as in 100 and 134, second section as in 24 and 113.

Pattern of *g* rare, with syncopated ending. Octave-leap between *f* and *g*.

Not noted in Zahn.

123

10   6   11   7   11   7   10   6

Iambic

1551, to text by Beza

2 stanzas—68 notes

Meter not elsewhere.

Doublet: $d = 36l$ and Nunc dimittis f.

Different patterns for all lines, most of them rare, including syncopated ending in b.

Not noted in Zahn.

124

10   10   10   10   10

Iambic

1551, to text by Beza

4 stanzas—50 notes

Meter not elsewhere, but in double form used in English by Sidney for Ps. 147.

Ratio of diatonic steps very high (93%). Pattern of *c* rare, with syncopated ending.

Taken into English and Scottish Psalters for the same Psalm, and into Ainsworth for Ps. 8 (patterns changed in English, but retained in the others). This tune, with line *c* omitted, is in present use as "Old 124th" or "Toulon."

Not noted in Zahn.

Sung in 1602 after the final repulse of the Savoyards in the so-called "Escalade."

125

9   6   6   9   9   5

Iambic

1551, to text by Beza

4 stanzas—44 notes

Meter not elsewhere.
Ratio of short notes low (41%).

From 1648 taken into Lutheran use. See Zahn, No. 2738, where the end of *e* is made syncopated instead of feminine.

8   8   8   8   9   9   8   8

Iambic

1551, to text by Beza

3 stanzas—66 notes

First line from a secular chanson. See Douen, I, 727.
Meter as in 148.
Repeat: $e = f$. Doublet: $g = 46c$.
Syncopated ending in a.

Quoted by Zahn (No. 5864), but without data of use.
Line g is read somewhat differently in Dutch Psalter, also by both
Zahn and Expert, as below. Paris version probably wrong.

127

For 127 see 117

128

7   6   7   6   7   6   7   6

Iambic

1544, to text by Marot

3½ stanzas—52 notes

Meter as in 130.

Ratio of short notes high (62%).

Taken into Scottish Psalter for the same Psalm (meter changed to C.M.D.).

From 1598 taken into Lutheran use. See Zahn, No. 5360.

129

10   11   10   11

Iambic

1551, to text by Beza

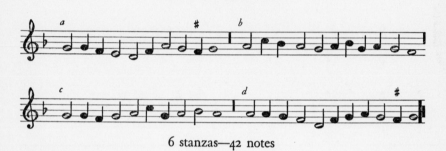

6 stanzas—42 notes

Meter not elsewhere.

Douen regards the mode as minor.

Different patterns for all lines. Those for *a* and *d* rare, both with syncopated endings.

Douen calls this tune one of the best.

Taken, unchanged, into Scottish Psalter for the same Psalm.

Not noted in Zahn.

130

Iambic

1539, to text by Marot

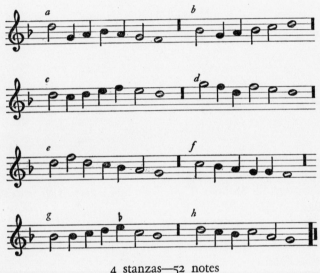

4 stanzas—52 notes

A Strassburg tune, but altered in 1542 and 1549. See Douen, I, 630–31, 634.

Meter as in 128.

Douen calls this tune one of the best.

Taken into the English and Scottish Psalters for the same Psalm, in the former with some change, in the latter unchanged; also into Ainsworth for Pss. 7 = 74 (meter changed to C.M.D.).

From 1587 taken into Lutheran use. See Zahn, No. 5352.

131

For 131 see 100

132

8   8   8   8   8

Iambic

1551, to text by Beza

12 stanzas—40 notes

Meter not elsewhere, but used in English by Sidney for Pss. 4 and 47. Ratio of diatonic steps low (71%).

Taken, unchanged, into Scottish Psalter for Ps. 36.
From 1848 taken into Lutheran use. See Zahn, No. 1785.

133

11   11   8   10   10   8

Iambic

1551, to text by Beza

2 stanzas—58 notes

Meter not elsewhere.
Doublet: $c = 105f$.
Rather free use of skips.

From 1853 taken into Lutheran use. See Zahn, No. 3171.

134

Iambic

1551, to text by Beza

3 stanzas—32 notes

Meter as in 100 and, doubled, as in 60. The latter used in English by
Sidney for 5 Psalms. First line from a secular chanson. See Douen, I, 727.
Only two patterns.

Douen calls this tune one of the best.

Taken into all the British Psalters, always for Ps. 100—whence the
traditional name "Old 100th." Patterns changed in English and Ainsworth, but unchanged in Scottish. See W. H. Havergal, *History of the
Old Hundredth Tune,* London, 1854, and article, "Old Hundredth," in
Grove's Dictionary.

From 1562 taken into Lutheran use. See Zahn, No. 368.

135

7   7   7   7   7   7

Trochaic

1562, to text by Beza

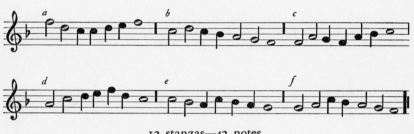

12 stanzas—42 notes

Meter as in 75, and used in English by Sidney for Ps. 16.
Doublets: $c = 150ab$ and $e = 75a$.
Only two patterns.

Not noted in Zahn.

7   7   7   7

Trochaic

1562, to text by Beza

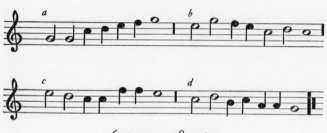

26 stanzas—28 notes

Meter not elsewhere, but used in English by Sidney for one section of Ps. 119 and, doubled, for Ps. 93. The shortest of the French meters. Only two patterns.

From 1711 taken into Lutheran use. See Zahn, No. 1181 (regarded as major, in C).

137

II   II   10   10   II   II

Iambic

1539, to text by Marot

5 stanzas—64 notes

A Strassburg tune (in D), slightly altered in 1549. First line from a secular chanson. See Douen, I, 631, 645, 729.

Meter not elsewhere, but used in English by Sidney for Ps. 138.

On pattern of *c,* see under Ps. 1.

From 1649 taken into Lutheran use (in early form). See Zahn, No. 3186 (using the 1539 reading of *e*).

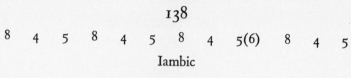

Iambic

1543, to text by Marot

4 stanzas—69 notes

Based almost throughout on a secular chanson. See Douen, I, 718–19. Meter not elsewhere.

Repeats: *abc = def* and *h = k*. Doublet: *j = 36ad*.

Ratio of short notes very low (38%). Patterns mostly unique. Lines *hi* and *kl* may be read as single lines. Octave-leap between *f* and *g*. The whole suggests a bell-theme.

Douen calls this tune one of the best.

From 1587 taken into Lutheran use. See Zahn, No. 8268.

139

For 139 see 30

140 = Decalogue

9 8 9 8

Iambic

1549 (Decalogue), to text by Marot
later (140), by Beza

13, 9 stanzas—34 notes

The third tune for the Decalogue, replacing one from the Strassburg books (1539, in D, with Kyrie) and another from Geneva (1542, without Kyrie). First line from a secular chanson. See Douen, I, 624, 644, 728.

Meter not elsewhere, but doubled in 66.

Ratio of diatonic steps very high (93%). Pattern of *a* unique.

Taken into English Psalter for Decalogue and into Ainsworth for Ps. 5 (both with meter changed to L.M.).

From 1576 taken into Lutheran use. See Zahn, No. 750.

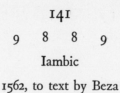

141

9   8   8   9

Iambic

1562, to text by Beza

11 stanzas—34 notes

Meter not elsewhere, except in second half of 17.
Ratio of diatonic steps low (70%). Patterns of *abc* rare.

From 1806 taken into Lutheran use. See Zahn, No. 749.

142

For 142 see 100

143

9 9 8 9 8

Iambic

1539, to text by Marot

12 stanzas—43 notes

A Strassburg tune, but somewhat altered in 1542 and 1549.
Meter not elsewhere.
Repeat: *b* = *d.*
Monotone openings in *b* = *d,* and imitation between *a* and *c.*

From 1657 taken into Lutheran use. See Zahn, No. 1816b.

144

For 144 see 18

IO   IO   IO   IO   II   II   II   II

Iambic

1562, to text by Beza

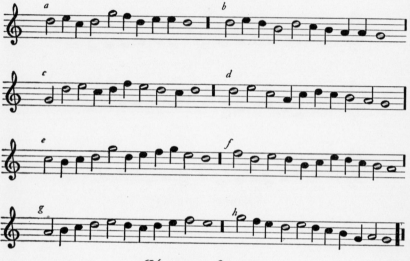

6½ stanzas—84 notes

Full meter not elsewhere, but first half as in 93. First half used in English by Sidney for Ps. 111 and second half for Ps. 121.

Pattern of *c* rare, with syncopated ending.

Not noted in Zahn.

146

8   7   8   7   7   7

Trochaic

1562, to text by Beza

8 stanzas—44 notes

Meter not elsewhere.

Doublet: $f = 61c$.

Only two patterns.

From 1648 taken into Lutheran use. See Zahn, No. 3613.

147

9   9   9   9   9   9   9   9

Iambic

1562, to text by Beza

10 stanzas—72 notes

Meter not elsewhere.

Doublet: $d = 83c$.

Ratio of diatonic steps low (70%). All lines with feminine endings.

Not noted in Zahn.

148

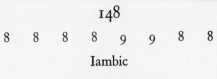

8   8   8   8   9   9   8   8

Iambic

1562, to text by Beza

5 stanzas—66 notes

Full meter as in 126 and first half as in 100 and 134.

Repeat: *e = f*. Doublet: *c = 80c*.

Patterns of *a* and *c* rare, the latter with syncopated ending. Octave-leap between *d* and *e*.

From 1643 taken into Lutheran use. See Zahn, No. 5866.

149

Iambic

1562, to text by Beza

4 stanzas—64 notes

Meter not elsewhere.
Douen regards the mode as minor.
Repeat: *e* = *f*. *Doublets:* *d* = 114*f* and *h* = 41*h*.
Pattern of *e* unique and those of *d* and *h* rare.

Not noted in Zahn.

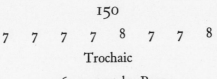

7   7   7   7   8   7   7   8

Trochaic

1562, to text by Beza

3 stanzas—58 notes

Full meter not elsewhere, but first half as in 136 and in Sidney. First line from a secular chanson. See Douen, I, 728.

Repeats: $a = b$ and $f = g$. Doublet: $a = 105c$.

Only two patterns.

From 1787 taken into Lutheran use. See Zahn, No. 6370.

Decalogue

For Decalogue see 140

Nunc Dimittis

6   6   7   6   6   7

Iambic

1549, to text by Marot

2 stanzas—38 notes

The second tune for this New Testament Psalm, replacing a Strassburg tune (in A, transposed), slightly changed in 1549. First line from a secular chanson. See Douen, I, 632–33, 636–37, 728.

Meter not elsewhere, but used in English by Sidney for Ps. 3.

Doublet: $f = 36l$ and $123d$.

From 1612 taken into Lutheran use. See Zahn, No. 2126.

This "Song of Simeon" is appended to the Psalms because regularly sung at the close of the Communion.

Index

Index

Index

Index

DUE DATE